CLEOPATRA'S NEEDLE:

WITH BRIEF NOTES ON

EGYPT AND EGYPTIAN OBELISKS.

By Erasmus Wilson

ISBN:978-1-63923-935-1

All Rights reserved. No part of this book maybe reproduced without written permission from the publishers, except by a reviewer who may quote brief passages in a review to be printed in a newspaper or magazine.

Printed: March 2023

Published and Distributed By:
Lushena Books
607 Country Club Drive, Unit E
Bensenville, IL 60106
www.lushenabks.com

ISBN: 978-1-63923-935-1

OUR EGYPTIAN OBELISK: CLEOPATRA'S NEEDLE.
ENGRAVED FROM A PHOTOGRAPH.

TO

HIS ESTEEMED FRIENDS,

CHARLES ALFRED SWINBURNE

AND

HENRY PALFREY STEPHENSON,

WHOSE JUDICIOUS COUNSELS
HAVE AIDED HIM IN CARRYING OUT
THE PROJECT OF SECURING

THE BRITISH OBELISK

TO

GREAT BRITAIN,

THIS LITTLE WORK IS AFFECTIONATELY
DEDICATED BY

THE AUTHOR.

PREFACE.

THE accompanying pages are intended as an introduction to the magnificent Egyptian Obelisk which is about to take its place among the monuments of London. This Obelisk was hewn in the renowned quarries of Syené, at the extreme southern boundary of Egypt, and was thence floated down the stream of the Nile to Heliopolis, the City of the Sun. It was erected, as one of a pair, in front of the seat of learning wherein Moses received his education, and stood in that position for about 1,600 years. Shortly before the Christian era it was conveyed to Alexandria, where it has remained until the present time, and is now on its voyage to the banks of the Thames. Its age, therefore, may be computed at upwards of 3,000 years.

At that early period, when other nations had not yet awakened into the dawn of civilisation, Egypt had made substantial progress in architecture and sculpture; and the British Obelisk may be taken as an admirable example of their excellence. The hieroglyphs which adorn its surface, inform us that it was erected by a powerful Pharaoh of the eighteenth dynasty, Thothmes III.; and that, 200 years later, it was carved with the name of another illustrious Egyptian potentate, Rameses the Great. The sculptures of Thothmes occupy the central line of each face of the shaft from top to bottom, and those of Rameses the side lines; so that, at a glance, we are enabled to compare the art of sculpture at periods of two centuries apart.

Heliopolis was the On of the Bible, and one of the cities of the Land of Goshen, where Abraham sought refuge when driven by famine out of Canaan. It was at Heliopolis that Joseph endured his slavery and imprisonment, and was rewarded by the Pharaoh of his day with the hand of Asenath, the daughter of Potipherah, a priest and ruler of On. Here he received in his arms his aged father Jacob, and Jacob fell on his neck and wept with joy at the recovery of his long-lost and well-beloved son: whilst in the neighbourhood of Heliopolis is still shown the venerable sycamore-tree, under which, according to traditional report, the Holy Family took shelter in their flight into Egypt.

These are some of the interesting associations which will crowd into the mind when we look upward at this colossal monolith, and of which it was once the silent spectator. Ancient Egypt, Egyptian enlightenment and refinement, scenes and acts of Bible history—are, as it were, realised by the presence of this stately object.

of art in the midst of our ancient, although, compared with itself, very modern, city. This, however, is not all; for our Obelisk was a witness to the fall of the Greek and the rise of Roman dominion in Egypt, and revives in our memory the brilliant exploits of Nelson at Aboukir, and the grievous loss sustained by Britain in the death of Abercromby, at Alexandria.

After the battle of Alexandria, in 1801, it had been the eager wish of the British army and navy to convey this Obelisk to England as a memorial of their victory. Weightier considerations frustrated their efforts.

In 1820, the matter was revived, and the Obelisk was formally presented by Mehemet Ali to the British nation, through His Majesty George IV.*

In 1822, a distinguished naval officer, Admiral W. H. Smyth, F.R.S., drew up a statement of plans by which the transport of the Obelisk might be accomplished; and Mehemet Ali offered to assist the undertaking by building a pier expressly for the purpose.†

In 1832, the propriety of making an endeavour to procure the Obelisk was discussed in Parliament, and supported by Joseph Hume, a sum of money being proposed for the purpose.

In 1867, Lieutenant-General Sir James Alexander directed his attention to the same subject, and read a Paper on the existing state of the Obelisk, before the

---

* See Appendix, p. 186. Letter from Consul Briggs to Sir Benjamin Blomfield.

† See Appendix, p. 199.

Royal Society of Edinburgh.* In 1875, he visited Alexandria for the purpose of ascertaining the actual condition of the Obelisk, and the possibility of getting it into British possession. A letter from Mr. Arthur Arnold to Lord Henry Lennox, First Commissioner of Works, dated April, 1876, and published in his book, entitled, " Through Persia by Caravan," exhibits one of the results of Sir James Alexander's exertions, and may be regarded as the most recent official report on the Obelisk question.†

While in Egypt, Sir James Alexander became acquainted with Mr. John Dixon, C.E., who had given considerable attention to the subject of the Obelisk and to the mode of its transport to England. Mr. Dixon had already made some successful explorations of the Great Pyramid, and had then brought his skill and experience, as a civil engineer, to bear on the practical question of the means and contrivance by which the transport of our Obelisk might be effected.

Such was the state of affairs in November, 1876, when Sir James Alexander first broached the subject to the author of these pages. Shortly afterwards the writer had an interview with Mr. John Dixon; succeeded by a conference, in which he was assisted by the judgment and advice of two valued friends—Mr. Charles Alfred Swinburne, of Bedford Row, and Mr. Henry Palfrey Stephenson, civil engineer. The conclusion

* Appendix, p. 190.
† See Appendix: Mr. Arnold's letter; p. 195.

arrived at in this conference was, that the undertaking was practicable; and an agreement was shortly afterwards (January 30th, 1877) signed, by which Mr. John Dixon engaged to set up the Obelisk on the banks of the Thames safe and sound.

The incidents of voyage, the shipwreck, the abandonment and recovery of the cylinder-ship " Cleopatra," together with her subsequent adventures, form an episode of surpassing interest, which has already been partly analysed in the journals of the day; but must now be left, for the completion of its history, until the Obelisk shall have been safely erected in London, on a site worthy of its antiquity and symbolical significance, and of the dignity of the metropolis of Great Britain. A happy chance already points to the precincts of Westminster Abbey, with its harmonious architectural and classical surroundings:—Westminster Hall, the Houses of Parliament, the Government Offices, the Horse-Guards, the Admiralty, Trafalgar Square, the Thames, and the most beautiful of its bridges, as a possible site; and in very truth, no better place can be found for it in our great city, even should Queen Anne graciously condescend to step from her pedestal at St. Paul's, to make way for her more ancient monumental companion.

In the compilation of these pages, the writer has availed himself of all the sources of information which his leisure has permitted him to consult; and he now takes the opportunity of expressing his especial obligations to the works of—Birch, Bonomi, Mariette, Sir Gardner Wilkinson, Sir Henry Rawlinson, George Rawlinson, Burton, Chabas, Pierret, Sharpe, Lane, Admiral Smyth, Rev. George Tomlinson, Parker, W. R. Cooper, Bayle St. John, Lady Duff Gordon, and Miss Edwards; although these authors represent only a portion of the writers in whose pages he has sought for instruction.

LONDON.
December, 1877.

CONTENTS.

	PAGE
ALEXANDER THE GREAT and Alexandria	1
The Cradle of Christian Theology	2
Succession of Persians, Greeks, and Romans in Egypt	3
The Ptolemies and the Cæsars	4
Queen Cleopatra	5
Cleopatra and Anthony	6
Shakspeare's Cleopatra	7
Queen Berenice: Coma Berenicis	9
Cleopatra's Needles	10
Inscription on the Bronze Supports of Cleopatra's Needles	11
Date of Erection of Cleopatra's Needles at Alexandria	12
Cæsarium; or Palace of the Cæsars	12
The British, or London Obelisk	13
The Pharaohs, Thothmes III. and Rameses II.	14
Signification of "Cartouche"	16
Age of the British Obelisk	17
Battle of Alexandria in 1801	17
Cleopatra's Needle in 1801	17
Burial of the British Obelisk with Obsequies	18
Obelisks and Needles	19
Monoliths of Syenite	20
Dimensions and Proportions of the Obelisk	21
The Paris Obelisk	22
Beauty and Durability of Syenite	23
Injury done by Sand-storms	24
Probable effect of British Climate	25
Time required to complete an Obelisk	25
Colossal Obelisks	26
Obelisks Carved when Erect	27
Pliny, the Younger, on Obelisks	28

CONTENTS.

	PAGE
Transport of Obelisks	29
Journey of the British Obelisk	29
Adoption of Obelisks by the Greeks	30
Export of Obelisks to Rome	31
Galleys of the Greeks and Romans	32
Maritime Prejudices of the Egyptians	33
Circumnavigation of Africa	34
The Emperor Constantine's Love of Obelisks	34
The Obelisk of Constantinople	35
Ruins of Alexandria	36
Pompey's Pillar at Alexandria	37
Diocletian's Title to Pompey's Pillar	38
CAIRO and the DELTA	40
Ismailia, a Health Resort	41
The Marvellous Nile	42
The Seven Cataracts of the Nile	42
Lady Duff Gordon and her " Letters from Egypt "	43
Christianity and Theology	44
West Bank of the Nile	45
Memphis and England's Colossus	46
The Great Pyramids of Geezeh	51
The Patriarch of Pyramids	52
The Colossal Sphynx	53
East Bank of the Nile	56
The Land of Goshen and Field of Zoan	56
Heliopolis and its Obelisk	58
Cartouches of the Pharaoh Usertesen	60
Temple of the Sun, dedicated to Ra and Tum	61
The Obelisk, Symbol of the Rising Sun and Life	63
Pharaoh's Needles	63
Napoleon's Address to the Army of the Pyramids	64
What have the Obelisks looked down upon	64
Abraham, Jacob, and Joseph in the Land of Goshen	65
Village of Matareeah; the Virgin's Tree	65
Hot Sulphur Springs of Helwân	66
Chronology of Ancient Egypt	68
Manetho, the Egyptian Chronologist and Priest	70
Analogies between Obelisk and Pyramid	72
Ornamentation of Obelisks	74
Scientific Knowledge evinced in their Construction	74
Carving of the Obelisk	75

	PAGE
Legend of the British Obelisk, by M. Chabas	76
The Flaminian Obelisk, of the Porta del Popolo	79
Legend of the Flaminian Obelisk	81
Standard of the King	82
The Grand Assemblies called Panegyries	86
Legend of the Paris Obelisk	87
Legend of the Alexandrian Obelisk	88
Moses and the British Obelisk	89
The Pharaoh of the Exodus	90
Era of Joseph in Egypt	90
Nile Voyage from Cairo to Thebes	90
Habits of the Crocodile	91
Geology of Egypt	92
The Mighty Ruins of Thebes	93
Memnonian Colossi; the Vocal Memnon	94
Earthquake before the Christian Era	96
Granite Colossus of Rameses the Great	98
Queen Hatasou's Western Obelisks	99
Village of Luxor	100
Tomb Architecture	100
Reign of the Mummies	101
The Pylon and Propylon	103
The Architect of Karnak	106
Colossal Statues and Sphynxes	107
Obelisk of Thothmes I. at Karnak	108
Obelisk of Hatasou, appropriated by Thothmes III.	108
Usertesen's Sanctuary	109
Lost Obelisks of Amenophis III.	110
The Luxor Obelisks	111
Obelisks of Rameses II.	113
Confusion of Thothmes and Hatasou, Seti and Rameses, and Rameses and Thothmes	114
Sacred Scarabæi and Manufacture of Antiques	117
Humanity of the Egyptians	119
Symbolism of the Scarabæus	120
Voyage from Luxor to As-souan	121
Unfinished Obelisk at As-souan	122
Mode of cleaving Obelisks from the Rock	123
"Beautiful Philæ" and "Pharaoh's Bed"	125
Obelisks of Philæ	126
The Bankes Obelisk	128
Resistance of Religious Faith to Theodosian Violence	131

CONTENTS.

	PAGE
Hieroglyphic Writing; how deciphered	133
The Rosetta Stone	134
Cartouches of Ptolemy and Cleopatra	135
Apotheosis of Egyptologists	137
USERTESEN and his Obelisks, Heliopolis and Biggig	138
Monolithic Monuments of the Hebrews	144
Abyssinian Obelisks	145
Inscription on the Biggig Obelisk	147
Obelisks of Thothmes I.	148
Obelisks of Queen Hatasou	148
Obelisks of Thothmes III.	149
Obelisk of Amenophis II.	152
Inscription on the Syon House Obelisk	153
Obelisks of Amenophis III.	154
Obelisks of Seti I., or Osirei	154
Obelisks of Rameses II.	156
Obelisks of Menephtah I.	158
Obelisks of Psammeticus I. and II.	159
Obelisks of Nectanebo I., or Amyrtæus	160
Obelisks of Nectanebo II.	162
Prioli Obelisk at Constantinople	164
Obelisk of Nahasb	166
Assyrian Obelisks	166
Ptolemaic Obelisks of Philæ	167
The Bankes Obelisk at Kingston-Lacy Hall	167
Albani Obelisk	168
Roman Obelisks	168
Obelisks at Alnwick	170
Obelisks in the Florence Museum	170
The Arles Obelisk	170
Egyptian Founders of Obelisks	172
Aggregate number of Obelisks	174
Bonomi's List of Altitudes of Obelisks	176
Classification and Distribution of Obelisks	178
Site of the British Obelisk	182

APPENDIX.

	PAGE
Extract from "Bombay Courier," 1802	185
Consul Briggs to the Right Hon. Sir Benjamin Blomfield, 1820; presentation of the Obelisk to George the Fourth, by Mehemet Ali	186
General Sir James Alexander; Paper read at the Royal Society of Edinburgh, 1868	190
Plan of Transport of the Obelisk, by Captain Boswell, R.N.	193
Report by Mr. Arthur Arnold, to Lord Henry Lennox, respecting state of Obelisk and Plans of Transport, 1876	195
Captain Methven's Plan of Transport, and Estimate	197
Admiral Smyth's Plans of Transport	199
Transport of the Luxor Obelisk to Paris, 1831-36	200
Carrick-a-Daggon Monument, in memory of General Browne Clayton, one of the Heroes of Alexandria	205
The British Ensign; half-mast, March 28th, in memory of our gallant and victorious Abercromby	207
Translation of the Legend of the British Obelisk, by Demetrius Mosconas	207
Ancient Heroic Poem in honour of Thothmes III., translated from the Tablet of Phtamosis	210
M. Mosconas' recent Work	213

ILLUSTRATIONS.

BRITISH OBELISK (*Frontispiece*).
ALEXANDRIAN OBELISK (*Vignette on Title-page*).

	PAGE
PARIS OBELISK	22
OBELISK AT CONSTANTINOPLE	35
POMPEY'S PILLAR AT ALEXANDRIA	37
THE COLOSSAL SPHYNX	54
OBELISK OF USERTESEN AT HELIOPOLIS	59
CARTOUCHES OF USERTESEN	60
STANDARD OF THE KING	82
MEMNONIAN COLOSSI, THE VOCAL MEMNON	94
PYLON OF A HOUSE OR TEMPLE	103
PROPYLON OF THE TEMPLE AT EDFOO	105
PLAN OF ORNAMENTATION OF THE ENTRANCE OF AN EGYPTIAN TEMPLE	111
SACRED SCARABÆI	116
ENGRAVED UNDER-SURFACE OF SCARABÆI	118
CARTOUCHES OF PTOLEMY AND CLEOPATRA	135
OBELISK AT AXUM IN ABYSSINIA	145
CARTOUCHES OF THOTHMES III.	150
CARTOUCHES OF RAMESES II.	156
BRITISH MUSEUM OBELISKS	161
OBELISK AT ARLES	171

CLEOPATRA'S NEEDLE.

MORE than twenty-two centuries ago—that is to say, about three hundred and thirty-two years before the birth of Christ—a Greek general, after a victorious campaign against the Persian rulers of Egypt, and a triumphant progress along the eastern boundary of the Delta (at that time the heart of the Egyptian kingdom), embarked in his galley on the Rosetta branch of the Nile, and swept down its stream to the Mediterranean Sea. Veering to the west, he steered along the African coast, and very soon came in sight of a small narrow island, called Pharos, lying at a short distance from the shore, and separated from it by a deep-sea channel capable of floating ships of heavy burden. This island served as a ready-made breakwater to the channel in-'side, and seemed intended to convert it into a natural harbour. It was on this very spot that the city of Alexandria sprung into existence, in obedience to the command of the victorious general already mentioned, who, indeed, was no less a personage than Alexander the Great, King of Macedonia, the first of a line of Greek kings who reigned over Egypt for three hundred years.

On the island of Pharos was laid the foundation of a magnificent lighthouse. The centre of the island was connected with the mainland by means of a mole, or causeway, three-quarters of a mile long; and this causeway contributed additional security to the harbour. Warehouses, docks, and streets, interspersed with temples, palaces, and monuments, sprung into existence with inconceivable rapidity; and that which originally was nothing more than a poor little fishing village, called Rhacotis, was speedily converted into the greatest and most flourishing city of the world, the chief seaport of Egypt, distinguished alike for its commercial prosperity and for its influence as a seat of learning. Here was established the celebrated library of Alexandria, the resort of philosophers from all the surrounding countries—from Greece, from Rome, from Babylon, from Jerusalem, from Persia, and from Palestine: here creeds were argued and debated; here Athanasius and Arian disputed; here the Holy Bible was translated into Greek (the common language of the people), for the benefit of the Alexandrian Jews; here the Evangelist Mark preached the gospel of Christ; and here the groundwork was laid of a future religion of brotherly love, moderation, and peace.

It was the habit of the human kind in those early ages—as, alas! is too often the case in the present day—to be puffed up by success and enfeebled by indulgence. So it fell out with the princes of Persia; for, in the latter years of their reign of two centuries in Egypt, the rulers became indolent and incompetent; they relied on others for the performance of duties which were inseparably their own; they enlisted an army of mercenaries in Greece; the mercenaries grew bold and powerful, and, in due time, seized on the possessions of their masters. The Greeks, in their turn, rushed forward to a similar fate; they conquered the world, and then, growing indifferent and luxurious, it was the easy task of the Romans to conquer them. Too enervated and too listless to maintain the greatness they had achieved, they purchased for their defence the help of the Roman soldiery; and the Roman legions, nothing loth, were not long before they occupied the throne of their employers. Three centuries saw the beginning and the ending of Greek rule in Egypt. Pompey and Julius Cæsar, fighting for the supremacy of the world, precipitated themselves on the oft-disputed battle-ground of Egypt; Pompey for refuge, Cæsar in pursuit; Pompey welcomed by false friends with the poniard, while, shortly afterwards, Cæsar fell by the hand of his colleagues and of his friend Brutus. And so it happened that Augustus, the renowned Roman emperor, became supreme sovereign of Egypt just thirty years before the Christian era; and Egypt was governed by the Romans for seven hundred years.

Ptolemy was the family surname of the Greek kings, and Cæsar that of the Roman emperors; so that it is not an uncommon thing to speak of the reign of the Ptolemies and the reign of the Cæsars; but as there were queens as well as kings among the Greeks, the prevailing name of the sovereign ladies was Cleopatra. The last of the Ptolemies left behind him, at his death, two sons and two daughters; both the sons were named Ptolemy, and the eldest daughter, Cleopatra.*

Cleopatra, says a popular author on the Greek dynasty (Samuel Sharpe), "had been a favourite name in Greece and with the royal families of Macedonia and Alexandria for at least four hundred years. What prettier name could be given to a little girl in her cradle, than to call her *the pride of her father*." Nevertheless Cleopatra was harshly dealt with by her brother: their father had directed that his eldest son and daughter should rule conjointly; but Ptolemy endeavoured to secure the throne for himself, and Cleopatra was obliged to fly the country. In this emergency Cleopatra sought and secured the assistance of Julius Cæsar; her brother was beaten in battle and drowned in his endeavours to escape the pursuit of the victorious army, and she was restored to the throne by Cæsar to rule conjointly with her younger brother.

After the death of Cæsar, Cleopatra fell into

* Cleopatra the famous, was the sixth Cleopatra.

disfavour with Mark Anthony. Mark Anthony was then at Tarsus, sovereign of the East, and tripartite ruler of the then known world. Tarsus is familiar to ourselves as the birthplace of the Apostle Paul, and the city which, in the infancy of Christianity, was enlightened by his teachings. It was situated on the river Cydnus; and here Cleopatra was commanded to appear before her powerful master Anthony, to meet the charges of misgovernment that had been made against her. "The beauty, sweetness, and gaiety of this young Queen," says Sharpe, "joined to her great powers of mind, which were all turned to the art of pleasing, had quite overcome Anthony; he had sent for her as her master, but he was now her slave. Her playful wit was delightful; her voice was an instrument of many strings; she spake readily to every ambassador in his own language; and was said to be the only sovereign of Egypt who could understand the language of all her subjects:—Greek, Egyptian, Ethiopic, Troglodytic, Hebrew, Arabic, and Syriac. With these charms, at the age of five-and-twenty, Anthony could deny her nothing."

Our compassion is beginning to be enlisted for the sovereign and the judge; for behold, the culprit approaches:—"She entered the river Cydnus with the Egyptian fleet, in a magnificent galley. The stern was covered with gold; the sails were of scarlet cloth; and the silver oars beat time to the music of flutes and harps. The Queen, dressed like Venus, lay under an awning embroidered with gold, while pretty dimpled boys, like Cupids, stood on each side of the sofa fanning her. Her maidens, dressed like sea-nymphs and graces, handled the silken tackle, and steered the vessel; as they approached the town of Tarsus, the winds wafted the perfumes and the scent of the burning incense to the shores, which were lined with crowds who had come out to see her land."

Shakspeare pursues the tempting theme in the same rapturous tone, having doubtless derived his history of Cleopatra, like Sharpe, from Plutarch.

"From the barge,
A strange invisible perfume hits the sense
Of the adjacent wharves. The city cast
Her people out upon her. And Anthony,
Enthroned in the market-place, did sit alone

> Whistling to the air; which, but for vacancy,
> Had gone to gaze on Cleopatra too,
> And made a gap in nature.
> Upon her landing, Anthony sent to her;
> Invited her to supper: she replied,
> It should be better he became her guest;
> Which she intreated: our courteous Anthony,
> Whom ne'er the word of "No" woman heard speak,
> Being barbered ten times o'er, goes to the feast,
> And for his ordinary pays his heart
> For what his eyes eat only."

The Roman soldier marvelled at the loveliness of his hostess and the splendour of her entertainment, and was not unwilling to repeat his visit. Each sumptuous feast surpassed in gorgeous profusion that which had gone before it, until a bet was laid that Cleopatra would give a banquet which should cost £60,000. She came to the entertainment adorned with two magnificent earrings of pearl, the largest in the world, and part of her suite of crown-jewels. In the midst of the feast an attendant set before her a cup of vinegar; she took a pearl from her ear and dropped it into the vinegar, and, when it was dissolved, she drank off the contents of the cup as a pledge to her distinguished guest. One of Anthony's friends, Plancus, adjudged that Anthony had lost the bet, and taking the other pearl from her ear, sent it to Italy, where it was cut in two and made into a pair of earrings for the statue of Venus, in the Pantheon of Rome.

A pleasant compliment had been paid, some two hundred years before that time, to another great Queen of Egypt, Berenice, the wife of Ptolemy Euergetes. Euergetes had been called to the wars, and Berenice, who was remarkable for a splendid head of hair, vowed, in her grief, that she would cut it all off and offer it as a sacrifice to the gods if her husband returned in safety. Ptolemy was victorious, the hair was dutifully cut off, and hung up in the Temple of Venus; after a time the hair disappeared, and Conon, the astronomer, being appealed to, declared that it had been carried off by Jupiter, who spreading it forth in the azure vault of heaven, had made of it a constellation of seven stars, which, to this day, is known as the "Coma Berenicis;" literally, Berenice's head of hair. There must have been grand prizes to be drawn in those lucky days by the fortunate: to be installed in the starry firmament could not otherwise be regarded than as a distinguished and lasting honour; and an astronomer who was desirous of standing well with the Court, had it in his power to pay an agreeable compliment. We can fancy Astronomer Conon, after a courteous reception at the palace, saying, as he took his leave, "Your name, Madam, shall be enrolled among the constellations, to shine brightly for ever and ever more." It was a pretty piece of scientific patronage, and convincing; for, of course, no further search was made for Berenice's curls.

These pleasant stories convey to us, as well as anything can, the admiration of the Egyptians for their lovely ones, and the ideal inspiration which associates itself with a name. We can no longer wonder that two superb obelisks, chiselled in the best period of Egyptian art, sculptured in the rose-coloured granite of the renowned quarries of Syené at the extremest limit of the kingdom, and set up in the midst of the regal city, made doubly lustrous by the presence of its beautiful Queen, and probably within the precincts of her favourite palace, should have received the name of Cleopatra's Needles; nor, that that name should be borne by them to all futurity.*

We assume, therefore, that the name of Cleopatra, associated with the two beautiful obelisks brought from Heliopolis, represents the popularity of the Queen, and the affectionate regard of her subjects, rather than any participation of herself in their transport or erection; and we are borne out in that presumption by Mr. Waynman Dixon's recent discovery of an inscription, engraved in Greek and Latin on the bronze supports of the standing obelisk. The inscription to which we refer reads as follows:—

Anno VIII. Cæsaris;—Barbarus, præfectus Ægypti, posuit;—Architectore Pontio.

"In the eighth year of Cæsar (Augustus), Barbarus, prefect of Egypt, erected this, Pontius being the architect."

---

* Cleopatra's Needle at Alexandria is the subject of the vignette on our title-page: it exhibits the infirm condition of the base of the obelisk; and it has been represented to the Egyptian government that, unless steps are taken to render it secure, it will probably share the fate of its fellow monolith. In the figure the pedestal is partially stripped of the earth and rubbish with which it is ordinarily covered.

Now, the eighth year of the reign of Cæsar Augustus, which he himself dated from the battle of Actium, was twenty-three years before the birth of Christ; and, consequently, seven years after the death of Cleopatra. It is not, however, at all improbable that Queen Cleopatra may have designed as well as contributed to the decoration of the palace during her lifetime, and that the setting-up of the obelisks may have been part of her plan. History likewise informs us that this grand palace of the Cæsars, the Cæsarium, was not finally completed until fifty years later— namely, in the reign of Tiberius. Mr. Sharpe says of it, that "it stood by the side of the harbour, and was surrounded with a sacred grove. It was ornamented with porticoes, and fitted up with libraries, paintings, and statues, and was the most lofty building in the city. In front of this temple they set up two ancient obelisks which had been made by Thothmes III., and carved by Rameses II.; and which, like the other monuments of the Theban kings, have outlived all the temples and palaces of their Greek and Roman successors. One of the obelisks has fallen to the ground, but the other is still standing, and bears the name of Cleopatra's Needle." Both obelisks, and consequently both Needles, are reported as having been standing at the end of the twelfth century.

And this brings us to the question:—What are these obelisks? and more particularly:— What is the British obelisk, of which its fellow at Alexandria is termed Cleopatra's Needle? The answer is:—that the sculptures on the four sides of the monument, its hieroglyphs or sacred writing, or more popularly, its picture-writing, declare it to be an invocation addressed to the deities of Egypt; a proclamation of the grandeur and deserts of the Pharaoh, by whom it is dedicated; his victories; his construction of temples and monuments; his love of justice, and his other exalted qualities, not forgetting the erection of this obelisk; the proclamation concluding with a prayer for health and a strong life. In the present instance the petitioner-in-chief is Thothmes III., and in the second place, Rameses II. Thothmes III., also called Thothmes the Great, was a distinguished Pharaoh, of a distinguished dynasty, the eighteenth, renowned for its grandeur and magnificence; and of his reign it has been said that Egypt could then plant the boundary of her territory wherever she chose. Rameses II. was likewise styled "Rameses the Great;" and by the Greek historian Herodotus, Sesostris: he was a Pharaoh of the nineteenth dynasty; in his early days a victorious soldier; and during the remainder of his long reign, a devoted cultivator of the arts of civilisation and peace. So that those who are discontent with the euphonious title of "Cleopatra's Needle," and prefer to be rigorously precise in their language, must contrive to familiarise their voice and their ear with the less euphonious title of "Thothmes-Rameses obelisk."

This obelisk bears evidence of having been constructed at the command of Thothmes, inasmuch as the legend of that monarch occupies the place of honour on its shaft—namely, the central portion of the face of the monument, extending from the top to the bottom; while the two sides of each face are devoted to that of Rameses. It is furthermore worthy of note, that about two hundred years must have intervened between the action of Thothmes and that of Rameses in relation to this obelisk. And consequently that the central and side columns of hieroglyphs represent periods of art of, at least, two centuries apart. It is also not a little singular that a king of vast renown, like Rameses the Great, should have preferred to publish the record of his own brilliant titles by the side of those of his distinguished predecessor, rather than raise a separate obelisk as an independent memorial of himself. Was it a submissive deference to the grandeur of his ancestor? Was it the ambition of linking his own name with that of the magnificent Thothmes? Or was it a part of that eccentricity of character which led him to stamp his escutcheon on several other works of his predecessors, and in some instances to obliterate their names in order to give his own a prominent place? In the present instance, we should be unwilling to treat of the combination as a blot, but would rather condone the offence—if such it be—and congratulate ourselves that the obelisk bears the insignia of two such grand Pharaonic personages. Thothmes III. and Rameses II. were undoubtedly the two greatest monarchs among the Pharaohs of Egypt; and the latter, besides being remarkable for the construction of temples and for his magnificent sculptures, was equally so for his eagerness to render his name universal. His cartouche* is to be met with extensively distributed all over Egypt, and also in those neighbouring countries which had been conquered by the Egyptian arms. He is the author of a considerable number of Egyptian obelisks; and his desire to occupy with his titles every vacant space of stone, is exhibited, not only by the writing on the British obelisk, but also by his appropria-

---

* Cartouche is a word introduced into Egyptology by Champollion; it signifies a scroll, or label, or escutcheon, on which the name of a Pharaoh is inscribed. Early Egyptologists had had their interest and curiosity awakened by observing the enclosure of certain hieroglyphs within an oval outline; and further research discovered that the ovals included hieroglyphs representing royal names and titles. The oval, or cartouche, is to be regarded therefore as the seal, or signet, or heraldic cypher of a king or potentate, and its presence on an obelisk or monument confers a right of authorship or proprietorship, and informs us to whom the monument belongs. The seal likewise typifies *renovation* and *immortality*, and on this account was selected as the badge of kings, to render immortality, which all Egyptians eagerly aspire to, the more secure. It is impossible to read Egyptian monuments correctly without a knowledge of the royal cartouches.

tion of two sides of two obelisks erected in the great temple of Karnak by Thothmes the First. With respect to the age of our own monument, it seems not improbable that the order for the British obelisk was given about sixteen hundred years before the Christian era; and consequently that its age, at the present time, may be taken to be about 3,500 years.

We have now lying before us an engraving, for which we are indebted to Captain Cotton, of Quex Park, in Thanet; an engraving published by Colnaghi, in May, 1803,* which bears the following legend:—" The obelisk at Alexandria, generally called Cleopatra's Needle, as cleared to its base by the British troops in Egypt, and similar to the one lying by it, intended to be brought to England. From the original drawing by Lieut.-Colonel Montresor, 80th Regiment, in the possession of the Right Honourable the Earl of Cavan, then Commanding-in-chief His Majesty's forces in Egypt." In this engraving, Cleopatra's Needle stands close to the sea, on a square pedestal mounted on three step-like plinths;

* The battle of Alexandria was fought within sight of Cleopatra's Needle, in March, 1801.

and is surrounded with broken arches, which may possibly have belonged to a magnificent temple or palace; while behind it are the towers and ruins of a part of the ancient city wall, and in the distance, stretching away into the sea, the promontory, on which stands the smaller lighthouse, or Pharillon. In recent photographs little is seen of these massive and extensive ruins; the Needle is sunk in a hole, the pedestal being lost to the sight, in a stonemason's yard; and the fallen obelisk is buried in the sand. "In 1849," says Mr. Macgregor, the celebrated canoe traveller, "this neglected gift was only half buried; but, in 1869, it was so completely hidden, that not even the owner of the workshop, where it lies, could point out to me the exact spot of its sandy grave." The Rev. Alfred Charles Smith corroborates the forlorn condition of the fallen obelisk at about the same date. "It is not only prostrate," he says, "but buried beneath a mass of rubbish; and, I doubt not, is now hopelessly covered in by the foundations of a house, for which preparations were being made at the time of our visit. We were so far benefited by the labours of the workmen, that we had a better view of the prostrate obelisk than has fallen to the lot of recent travellers, inasmuch as, in excavating the ground at this spot, the labourers had uncovered nearly the entire length of the recumbent granite, and as they were just about to fill-in the earth around, I suppose we were the last tourists who have looked in upon the open grave of this renowned relic, * * * * though I am bound to add it is the most dilapidated, weather-worn, and ill-conditioned of all its brethren on the banks of the Nile." *Nous verrons.*

The term "Needle" is familiar to our ear as designating a pointed shaft soaring upwards into the sky. In this sense we adopt it as the name of certain pointed rocks rising perpendicularly out of the sea, such as the "Needles" of the Isle of Wight; and it has been similarly applied to two of the obelisks of Heliopolis, Pharaoh's Needles, which were removed by Constantine. It is a term peculiarly suitable to the obelisk, which, according to Johnson, is "a magnificent high piece of solid marble or other fine stone, having usually four faces, and lessening upwards by degrees till it ends in a point like a pyramid." The term obelisk is

of Greek origin, derived from the word
"*obelos*," a spit; conveying the idea of a
pointed implement; but its Arab synonym is
still more explicit—namely, "*meselleh*," which
literally means "a packing needle or skewer;"
the ancient Egyptian name of obelisk being
tekn.

The Egyptian obelisks have two other important features:—first, they are monoliths, and secondly, they are hewn out of the quarries of rose-coloured granite of Syené. By monolith is meant "a single stone," from the Greek words "monos," one or single, and "lithos," a stone, and is intended to signify that the object is formed of a single piece; therefore we have good reason for our wonder when we see before us a stately shaft of granite consisting of a single piece, very little short of a hundred feet in height, and weighing nearly two hundred tons.[*]

The Egyptian obelisk has another peculiarity; it is rarely uniform in breadth on all its four sides; the opposites agree, but the neigh-

---

[*] The real weight of the British obelisk is 186 tons, seven hundredweight, two stones, eleven pounds; and its cubic measurement 2,529 feet.

Dimensions of the Obelisk.

bouring sides differ. This difference is clearly not intentional, but a possible consequence of the method of splitting so gigantic a shaft from its mother-rock. The British obelisk, for example, measures 7 feet 5 inches in breadth at its base on one side, and close upon 8 feet (7 ft. 10½ in.) on the adjoining side—a difference of five inches and a-half; while similar measurements of the Alexandrian obelisk give 7 feet 9¾ inches, and 8 feet 2¼ inches—a difference of only two inches and a-half. The proper proportions of the shaft of an obelisk, exclusive of its pyramidion, are said to be ten times the breadth of the base. Now if we apply this rule to the British obelisk, its height should be nearly eighty feet, whereas its extremest height, from the base to the point, is *sixty-eight feet five inches and a-half*. From its base of 7 feet 5, or 7 feet 10½ inches, it tapers gradually upwards to a breadth of 4 feet 10 inches, or 5 feet 1 inch; and then contracts into a pointed pyramid of 7 feet 6 inches high. The Alexandrian obelisk is hardly so tall as the British obelisk, and measures 67 feet 2 inches. But when the British obelisk shall have been raised on its

The Paris obelisk, brought from Luxor, and now standing in the Place de la Concorde. A work of Rameses II.

pedestal of ten feet square, and mounted on plinths, the monument will then have an altitude of over eighty feet. Comparing it with the Paris obelisk, the latter is seventy-six feet and a-half in height, consequently nearly eight feet higher than the British obelisk: whereas one of Pharaoh's Needles, set up before the Lateran Church in Rome, was originally more than 108 feet high; but having lost part of its base, at present measures 105 feet 7 inches.

The rose-coloured granite of Syené, the so-called "Syenite," has acquired a world-wide reputation for its beauty of colour, the lustre of its polish, and its hardness of texture. In the dry climate of Upper Egypt, where a rainy day occurs only four or five times in the year, this granite may be said to be absolutely indestructible; and therefore it is that the Egyptian sculptures and obelisks, more than four thousand years old, come down to us almost as fresh as if they had just issued from the workman's hand. The engraving of the hieroglyphs is often several inches in depth, its hollows carefully polished, and the work comparable to the delicate carving of a gem.

But although the Egyptian climate deals tenderly with these beautiful objects, the sand-storms are not so merciful: showers of sand are often precipitated with the violence of small shot against the polished stone; and the sharp particles of sand, by successive battery, leave their impression on the surface: at first the polish alone is blurred; but by degrees the picture-writing itself is worn away. This is apparent on the Alexandrian obelisk, of which the two sides exposed to the fury of the land-storms are seriously corroded, while the sea-face is but little injured. The British obelisk shows similar marks of wear from causes of the same kind, but has further to complain of the rapacity of travellers, who have damaged it considerably in their endeavours to carry away fragments of so brilliant a memorial of ancient times. The angles of the shaft have been chipped in many places; and as a refinement of mischief, even the perpendicular sides of some of the hieroglyphs have likewise been chiselled away. When we come to the patriarch of obelisks at Heliopolis, that of King Usertesen I., we shall find that the Nile has been busy with its sheen, and has left his mark of annual overflow on the lower part of its shaft; whilst elsewhere we have the account of a fragment of an ancient obelisk set up in the midst of a garden, in the perfumed atmosphere of luxuriant flowers, in which the wild bees have puttied up the channels of the hieroglyphics with their tenacious combs. But another and a graver trial is in waiting for our obelisk:—How will it accommodate itself to the climate of the British metropolis? It will endure: of that we can have no doubt; neither will it fail in our respect and admiration even when it has lost some of its pristine loveliness, and has submitted to harmonise its tone with the dulness of its surroundings.

The hewing, the carving, and the burnishing of one of these huge monoliths, under any circumstances, must have been a laborious undertaking, and have required a considerable period for its completion. Thus we are informed that one of the obelisks of Heliopolis, one of Pharaoh's Needles, a work of Thothmes III., occupied thirty-six years in its elaboration. It is the tallest of its race, and now stands as a memorial of the Emperors Constantine and Constantius, in front of the

Lateran Church at Rome; whereas another obelisk, now standing at Karnak (also of the Thothmes period, but executed under the direction of Queen Hatasou, daughter of Thothmes I., and sister of the second and third Thothmes), is stated, in an inscription on its base, to have been, with its fellow, hewn from the quarry and erected in the short period of seven months. Queen Hatasou's obelisk is the second in altitude of the obelisk family, measuring 97 feet 6 inches;* while that of St. John Lateran, when entire, measured about 108 feet.

It has been suggested as probable that the obelisk was brought, in the rough state, to the spot where it was to stand, and that it was smoothed and polished there previously to its erection. And a further question arises:—Was it erected plain, and afterwards carved in the erect position, or was it carved before it was set up? If the former of these suppositions be admitted, then the hewing and erecting of

* Queen Hatasou's obelisk has been stated to be 108 feet high; but M. Mariette, who makes this statement in one of his books—in a more recent work, calls it as above, 97 feet 6 inches, which is probably correct.

the pair of monoliths in seven months is not so marvellous, especially when we call to mind the vast number of artificers always at the command of the Egyptian Government. There is clear evidence that carving after erection was practicable, and not unusual; for it must have been in the erect position that the side columns of engraving were added to the British obelisk by Rameses, and no doubt that also on the Thothmes obelisk at Karnak. The inscription on the base of Queen Hatasou's obelisk affords an additional argument in proof of the ornamentation of the column being subsequent to erection, inasmuch as it informs us that the whole shaft was gilt from top to bottom; and although, at the present time, all trace of gold has vanished, the surface of the stone bears evidence of having been left rough, as if prepared to receive a thin coating of plaster such as was in common use among the builders of the temples, when painting was resorted to; the hollows of the carvings being left smooth and polished. The same inscription likewise states that the obelisk was capped with gold, the spoils of war, wrested from the enemies of the country.

Pliny the younger, after mentioning the Syenite granite as sown with fiery spots, remarks, that a certain king of Egypt was admonished in a dream to set up obelisks. " The kings of Egypt," he says, " in times past, as it were upon a strife and contention one to exceed another, made of this stone certain long beames, which they called obelisks, and the very Egyptian name implieth so much." Rameses, he observes, " pitched on end another obeliske which carried in length a hundred foot, wanting one, and on every side four cubits square." * "It is said that Ramises above named kept 2,000 men at work about this obeliske;" and to secure its safe erection, " caused his own son to be bound to the top thereof. * * * Certes, this obeliske was a piece of work so admirable, that when Cambyses had won the city where it stood, by assault, and put all within to fire and sword, and burnt all before him as far as to the very foundation and underpinning of the obeliske,

---

* This may have been one of the Luxor obelisks, notwithstanding the alleged difference of height; since even, at the present day, the figures of Egyptologists are remarkably unreliable.

commanded expressly to quench the fire; and so, in a kind of reverence, yet unto a mass and pile of stone, spared it, who had no regard at all of the city besides." *

When the obelisk was completed at Syené, the next step was that of its removal to the spot where it was destined to stand. This was usually effected by excavating beneath it a dry dock, and fixing therein two large barges. When all was properly adjusted, the water was let into the dock, and as the barges rose they lifted up their burden, and formed a raft, which was then floated down the stream of the Nile. In the case of the British obelisk, the destination of the raft was Heliopolis, a distance, as the crow flies, of nearly 600 miles: subsequently, as we know, the obelisk was conveyed to Alexandria, adding nearly 150 miles more, and making a real total of 730 miles. And if to these figures we allow 3,000 for the journey home, we have reason to hail our obelisk as a not inconsiderable traveller.

* "The Historie of the World," commonly called the "Natural Historie of C. Plinius, secundus." Translated into English by Philemon Holland, Doctor of Physicke; 1634: book 36, chap. 8.

We can hardly be surprised that the Greeks and the Romans should have been fascinated with the delicate beauty of the obelisks, and should have desired to possess them. Two hundred and eighty-four years before the birth of Christ, Ptolemy Philadelphus built a tomb for his wife Arsinoë at Alexandria, which he enriched with an obelisk fifty-six feet high. The obelisk had been cut, as usual, in the quarry of Syené during the reign of the last of the Egyptian Pharaohs, Nectanebo II.; it had not been engraved, but its date may be stated as about six hundred years before the Christian era. The architect, Satyrus, transported it in a somewhat similar manner to that already described. "He dug a canal to it as it lay upon the ground, and moved two heavily-laden barges underneath it. The burdens were then taken out of the barges, and as they floated higher they raised the obelisk off the ground. He then found it a task as great, or greater, to set it up in its place; and this Greek engineer would surely have looked back with wonder on the labour and knowledge of mechanics which must have been used in setting up the obelisks, colossal statues, and pyramids which he saw scattered over the country." It was erected, according to Pliny, "in the haven of Arsinoë * * * but for that it did hurt to the ship docks there, one Maximus, a governor of Egypt under the Romans, removed it from thence into the market-place of the said city (Rome), cutting off the top of it, intending to put a finial thereupon gilded, which afterwards was forelet and forgotten." This description corresponds with that of the obelisk now standing behind the church of St. Maria Maggiore, in Rome, which is wanting both in inscription and pyramidion; but its present height is stated to be only 48 feet 5 inches, in lieu of 56 feet. This latter circumstance may be accounted for on the supposition of its having been broken before it was finally erected at Rome—an accident by no means unusual with the Roman obelisks—and by the probable squaring of its base for the purpose of securing a steadier foundation.

The Emperor Augustus, the conqueror of the last of the Ptolemies, and pioneer of the Roman dynasty, who took possession of the throne of Egypt thirty years before the Christian era, signalised his artistic taste by sending four beautiful obelisks to Rome: one of the period of Seti I. and his son Rameses II.; one of that of Psammeticus II.; and two without inscription or pyramidion, of which one is ascribed to Nectanebo. These obelisks now occupy places of honour in Rome— one in the Piazza del Popolo, the elegant Flaminian obelisk; one on the Piazza de Monte Citorio; one behind the church of St. Maria Maggiore; and the remaining one in the Piazza Quirinale. That on the Monte Citorio was originally planted in front of the church of St. Lorenzo in Lucina, where it acted as the gnomon or pointer of a sun-dial erected by Augustus; and the two plain obelisks were set up in front of his mausoleum.

The means employed by Augustus for the transport of these obelisks was a galley propelled by 300 oars-men. The war-ships of the Greek and Roman dynasties were sometimes of imposing magnitude and strength, and were furnished with a number of rams. One of these ships "was 420 feet long, and fifty-seven feet wide, with forty banks of oars. The longest oars were fifty-seven feet long, and weighted with lead at the handles, that they might be the more easily moved. This huge ship was to be rowed by 4,000 rowers; its sails were to be shifted by 400 sailors, and 3,000 soldiers were to stand in ranks upon deck. There were seven beaks in front, by which it was to strike and sink the ships of the enemy. The royal barge in which the king and Court moved on the quiet waters of the Nile, was nearly as large as this ship of war. It was 330 feet long, and forty-five feet wide."

This maritime power of Egypt calls to mind two leading prejudices of the ancient Egyptians, which very much influenced their destiny: they were averse to change, preferring, in all things, to remain as they were, rather than risk the uncertainty of reform; and, secondly, they had a religious horror of the ocean, believing it to be a breach of the divine law to endeavour to subdue it, and attempt to navigate it. Therefore, when we hear of ships from Alexandria finding their way through the Pillars of Hercules (otherwise the Straits of Gibraltar) to England, we recognise at once the adventure of neighbouring nations, particularly that of the Phœnicians, who traded with Cornwall, exchanging wheat for metal more than five hundred years before the Christian era. The last of the Egyptian kings, Nectanebo II., made a struggle against this ancient prejudice, and fitted up a fleet in the Red Sea, manned by Phœnicians. His ships, steering steadily to the south, and afterwards following the line of the coast, succeeded in rounding the Cape of Good Hope, and reaching the Straits of Gibraltar, and so accomplished the circumnavigation of Africa. The voyage lasted between two and three years, and the captain returned in safety to Egypt, but without his ships; he consequently failed to obtain credit for, or belief in, his success.

Constantine, the first Christian among the emperors of Rome, conveyed to Byzantium, as a decoration for his new city of Constantinople, an obelisk of the period of Thothmes III., which now graces the Atmeidan, or Hippodrome: it stood originally at Heliopolis, and was one of the Needles of Pharaoh. He likewise, in all probability, sent to Arles the obelisk which is now standing in that city. It was found, in later times, grown over with

The obelisk at Constantinople, standing in the open space of the Atmeidan, near the church of St. Sophia. It is square at the base, and supported at the corners upon four small metallic blocks, which rest on a narrow pedestal. Its present height is only fifty feet; but seeing that it was originally the companion at Heliopolis of the great obelisk of St. John Lateran, it must therefore have been shortened, possibly as a consequence of accident. It was conveyed to Byzantium by Constantine, and erected on its present site, probably by Theodosius. The figure is not to be commended for its exactness; the monument is evidently much too tall. The mosque in the background is that of the Sultan Achmet.

bushes, and partly buried in garden a at the port of La Roquette. Charles the Second and Catherine de Medicis ordered its disinterment, and it was erected at Arles, as a memorial of Louis the Great, in the year 1676. Constantine directed the removal of another obelisk from Heliopolis, and this he also intended for Constantinople; but dying previously to its arrival at Alexandria, it was conveyed to Rome by his son Constantius. This latter is the beautiful obelisk set up in the Piazza of St. John Lateran at Rome: it is the tallest obelisk known; and although it has lost three feet of its base, measures at present 105 feet 7 inches. It bears the signets of Thothmes III. and Thothmes IV., and is the obelisk previously mentioned as having occupied thirty-six years in the preparation. The temple of Serapis at Alexandria formerly possessed two fine obelisks, but both have now disappeared; they, probably, may also have found their way to Rome. The ruins of this temple were called the citadel; and all that remains of both is Pompey's Pillar, which was erected in one of the principal courts of the temple.

Pompey's Pillar at Alexandria.

Pompey's Pillar is a magnificent column, placed on a hillock just outside the walls of the old town. It is cut out of red syenic granite; is beautifully polished, and is said to be the largest monolithic pillar in the world; its total height, according to Captain Smyth,

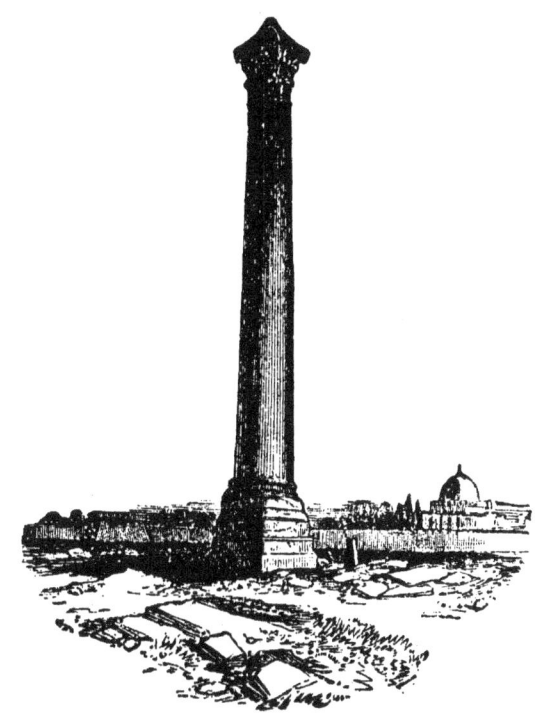

Pompey's Pillar at Alexandria.

being 99 feet 4¾ inches; or, in round numbers, 100 feet, including the pedestal; its girth, near the base, being nearly 28 feet. It is surmounted with a Corinthian capital, of a differently coloured granite from that of the shaft, and of inferior workmanship, and stands on a short stump of a broken obelisk about four feet high, inverted, and built into the pedestal; the surface of the obelisk being covered with hieroglyphs. The column was ascended by the French in 1798, and by Captain Smyth in the spring of 1822. Captain Smyth wished to ascertain its qualification for astronomical purposes; but found it too unsteady for delicate observations; and, moreover, that it had an inclination to the southwest, in the direction opposite to that of the prevailing north-east wind. It has an inscription on the pedestal, which cost much time and perseverance to make out,* and was at length deciphered as follows:—

"Consecrated to the adorable Emperor Augustus Diocletian, the tutelar divinity of Alexandria, by Pontius, prefect of Egypt."

* A French writer, referring to the decipherment of this inscription, which, as it appears, was an onerous undertaking, observes:—"This scientific labour fell to the lot of two British soldiers, Captain Dundas and Lieutenant Desarde, and to them we are indebted for the discovery of 'a page of history, and a splendid page.'"

Siege of Alexandria. 39

This inscription clearly settles the personality of the column, and is an answer to those by whom it has been called " The Pillar of Severus," and " The Pillar of Hadrian." One author believes that it might have been erected by Ptolemy Euergetes, as a record of the recovery of some thousands of pictures and statues which had been carried off by Cambyses. But the true story appears to be this:—In the year 297 of the existing era, Egypt had risen in rebellion against her rulers, and Alexandria, always contumacious, was subdued by Diocletian after a siege of eight months. Diocletian, riding among the obstructions which encumbered the fallen city, was nearly thrown from his horse. His escape from accident doubtless prompted a grateful feeling in his heart towards the Father of Mercies, and he erected this pillar as a witness of his faith, surmounting it with a statue of his horse, which has long since disappeared. Nevertheless, the ancient prejudices of our affections are ever ready to spring forth, like buried seeds in a garden; and a deep-felt regard for the old consul, Pompey, who had been so treacherously assassinated on the shores of Egypt, now competes with the better claims of Diocletian for the honour of this magnificent memorial; just as the obelisks of Alexandria will, to the end of time, ever be remembered in association with the memory of Cleopatra.

We have advanced at present no further than the portal of the country which stands supreme in the production of these interesting relics of former grandeur, the obelisks; and yet we have made acquaintance with nearly twenty which have emigrated from their native land. Rome is the fortunate possessor of ten; France, of two; Constantinople, of two; and England, of Cleopatra's Needle and four or five smaller ones. Let us now take a step further onwards, and visit them in their parental home. Four hours and a-half in the railway-train (express) suffice to transport us from Alexandria to Cairo, a distance of 130 miles. Cairo, the queen of Eastern cities, is the present metropolis of Egypt, the seat of its government, and the residence of its ruler, Ismail Pasha, the Khedive, Viceroy of the Sultan of Turkey. It is situated at the apex or head of the Delta, and forms the nob of the fan, of which the ribs, radiating northwards towards the sea, are the seven branches of the Nile; or, we may prefer to regard it as one of the three points of the triangle termed Delta; Alexandria and Port Said, 140 miles apart, occupying the other two points. Port Said, indeed, is bidding fair to become the rival of Alexandria, and will grow in importance with the Suez Canal, of which it is the entrance. Already we hear of the defences of the seaboard between Alexandria and Port Said, and the protection of a work which is identified with the intrinsic prosperity of England. An Egyptian Bournemouth or Torquay, in the meantime, has established itself on the line of the canal, and invalids are already migrating for health to Ismailia, to luxuriate in the balmy and exhilarating climate of Egypt.

Cairo is comparatively a modern city, being 1,200 years the junior of Alexandria, and possesses few traces of antiquity. A fragment of an obelisk helps to pave one of its entrance-gates—alas! to what base uses fallen!—probably a work of Usertesen, of Thothmes, or of Rameses. But if we turn our back upon the Delta, the land of prolific produce, the battle-field of many centuries, and the grave of innumerable ancient cities, and gaze towards the south, we see before us that wonderful river, which, rising in the bosom of Africa, and bursting through the granite rocks of Syené—the As-souan, or gate of Egypt—precipitates itself, a foaming cataract,* into the valley of Egypt, and pursues its meandering course, without tributary and without bridge, for more than 600 miles in a straight line from Syené to Cairo. It is a river of poetry

* The fall of the Nile at Syené, or As-souan, is termed the first cataract, in consideration of its being the first of seven similar falls which occur in the course of that river. It is in reality the only fall in Egypt, the second being in Nubia, 200 miles higher up. Strictly speaking, it is not a cataract, but a succession of rapids three miles in length, and studded with rocks. The ascent of the Dahabeeyah is made without danger between these rocks and through the more practicable channels; but the descent brings to view dangerous cataracts of considerable force and volume, demanding much experience and ability on the part of the captain to shoot them with safety, and a well-built boat to bear the shock. Hence a prime care of the traveller, before starting from Cairo, is to secure a vessel capable of encountering the risks of the cataract. The second cataract, from its greater extent and more numerous rocks, is practically impassable. The abundance of the rocks in its bed has suggested for it the Arab expression of "the belly of stone."

and of fertility; for nine months of the year the northern breeze (the Etesian wind) blows against its stream from early morning until night, to waft the travellers, in the sylph-like Nile-boat, called Dahabeeyah, through their journey of health and recreation. At night the boat is moored for its rest; the wind is lost in sleep, but wakens to its duties in the early morn; while rain is a thing almost unknown. In the month of June the Nile rises at Syené; and during August, September, and October, the low flat land of the Delta is converted into a sheet of water, which diffuses richness and fruitfulness throughout the grimy soil.

Lady Duff Gordon, in her agreeable "Letters from Egypt," under date 1863-5 (the time of the mutiny), tells us how she passed a winter at El-Uksur, residing in the French house—a ruinous building, which had been occupied by the French officers who had charge of the expedition for conveying the Luxor Obelisk to Paris. She takes especial note of "a whole wet day," as an event unknown in Thebes for ten years. During her residence in Upper Egypt, she watched the annual rising of the Nile, and remarks that the water was at first green, and soon after blood-red; the apparent colour being, in both cases, probably due to refraction of light. Some authors speak of the waters of the Nile as being greenish-brown, and brown; and others as yellow. Mr. A. C. Smith calls the Nile "yellow, muddy, and sluggish:" when filtered it throws down a considerable deposit of mud, containing an abundance of organic matter, but is then sweet, soft, and peculiarly palatable. As an example of Egyptian veneration for the grand old river, Lady Duff Gordon observes, that whenever a marriage is celebrated, and the bridegroom has "taken the face" of his bride—that is, has looked upon that which is habitually concealed from view, namely, the face—she is conducted to the river bank to gaze upon the Nile.

Lady Duff Gordon, who had a warm heart for every living thing, tells us a story which is worthy of reflected thought even in the sunny atmosphere of the mysterious obelisk. She had a Nubian child offered her as a slave: when she went to look after the gift, she found it among the pots and kettles, cuffed and ill-treated by every one, saving perhaps only the dog. She brought it to her room, warmed it in her bosom, dressed it, and made it comfortable; nay, indulged it, and won its confidence—in the world's language, its love. The child wept sorely when its good and kind mistress returned home to England; but the mistress provided tenderly for her adopted, and secured its comforts during her absence. When Lady Duff Gordon returned to Egypt, the little negress held a prominent place in her thoughts: she took it again into her guardianship; but the child was no longer the same; she was self-willed, she was disobedient; the slave had learnt— alas! too readily—to despise her mistress! holding her to be an accursed Christian, a giaour. Verily the father of all evil is ignorance, which for ever stands sentry over the tree of knowledge. Need we not all— charity?

On our right hand, as we look forward into the south, is the site of ancient Memphis, founded by Menes, first of the kings of Egypt. Here stood once a magnificent temple, dedicated to the god Ptah, the representative of

"Creation;" but at present, a collection of ruinous tombs, together with some broken colossal statues, partly engulphed in sand, are all that remains of its original greatness. One of these relics, a colossal statue of Rameses the Great, is believed to belong to England, and only awaits removal to a fitting resting-place. It has the reputation of being beautifully carved in fine sandstone, but is corroded and blackened by the action of water, in which it lies immersed at every rising of the Nile. Dean Stanley, in allusion to this same locality, observes:—

"One other trace remains of the old Memphis. It had its own great temple, as magnificent as that of Ammon at Karnak, dedicated to the Egyptian Vulcan, Ptah. Of this not a vestige remains. But Herodotus describes that Sesostris—that is, Rameses—built a colossal statue of himself in front of the great gateway. And there, accordingly, as it is usually seen by travellers, is the last memorial of that wonderful king, to be borne away in their recollections of Egypt. Deep in the forest of palms before described, in a little pool of water left by the inundations,

which year by year always cover the spot, lies a gigantic trunk, its back upwards. The name of Rameses is on the belt. The face lies downwards, but is visible in profile and quite perfect, and the very same as at Ipsambul, with the only exception that the features are more feminine and more beautiful, and the peculiar hang of the lip is not there." Of the immediate neighbourhood he says:—
"For miles you walk through layers of bones and skulls, and mummy swathings, extruding from the sand, or deep down in shaft-like mummy-pits; and amongst these mummy-pits are vast galleries filled with mummies of ibises in red jars, once filled, but now gradually despoiled."

Mr. Bayle St. John, who, for his heresies in Egyptology and floutings of obelisks, almost puts himself out of the pale of quotation, has a word to say about the colossal statue at Memphis, which is worth noting as expressing the views of the tranquil lounger rather than those of the hurried traveller. In his "Village Life in Egypt" (1852), he says:—
"After a long ride, a reedy pond covered with wild ducks, a stone bridge, and some

sluice-gates, warned us that we were approaching the buried skeleton of Memphis. Vast mounds rose on all hands among the palm-trees, evidently the remains of a continuous wall of unburnt bricks, and we were soon moving along the sward-covered sloping banks of the lake, in which the palm-groves that cover the site of the ancient city, admire their graceful forms. Behind, in a hollow in the ground, was the colossal statue which we had come to see. It lay on its face, its pensive brow buried in mud, and part of the features concealed by some still-lingering water. The Arabs call it Abu-l-Hôn, and say it is a giant king, turned by God, 'in ancient times and seasons past,' into stone for some great crime. They are not at all astonished at the interest felt by infidels in this petrified sinner, because we come of the same accursed stock, and feel deserving of the same punishment. A few hovels rising amidst the palm-trees near the statue, bear the name of Mitraheny, formerly a place of some importance, but now not even wearing the appearance of having seen better days. Here dwelt old Fatmeh, the guardian of the fallen monarch, who could have told strange things of his history, had any been curious enough to question her." On another occasion he says: " The following morning I went to visit my old friend Abu-l-Hôn, the father of terror, who still lies nose down in the hollow at Mitraheny, as he has lain for thousands of years. It is a pretty long walk, first through the grove to Bedreshein, and then along the winding gisr to the great grove of Mitraheny. The place is a beautiful one. A small lake in the cooler time of the year, before the thirsty sun comes and drinks up every scrap of moisture except the river, spreads in the centre of the grove, dotted with little islands, that multiply as the season advances. A close greensward, from which thousands of palms spring at regular intervals, creeps down on all sides after the receding water * * * immense numbers of aquatic birds make it their resort. About sunrise it is perfectly covered with wild ducks, which come back regularly at evening after dark. Herons dot its shores all day, admiring, it seems, their ungainly forms, which it reflects; and a variety of little birds, peculiar to the country, flutter with dancing flight about its archipelago of sedgy islands. * * * The statue was near the southern extremity of the lake. During many years it was under the protection of an old dame, who entirely devoted herself to its custody. Formerly, various consuls gave her a little pension; but this gratuity was at length withdrawn, and she subsisted on the voluntary gifts of travellers, always believing, however, that the English nation would at length hear of the care she took of their property, and reward her by a pension of £5 a year. Such was the extent of her ambition. In this hope she lived and died. I found her son occupying the same post, and indulging in the same expectations. He had inherited her little house and some sheep, and professed to do nothing but watch over the comfort of the petrified king in the hole. * * * It would be good, instead of spending a great deal of money in carrying *an ugly obelisk** to England, to devote a little to raising this extraordinary statue on its old base, otherwise, some fine day we shall hear

* And this to your friend, Bayle? Hast forgotten thy school lessons:—Quot homines tot sententiæ.

of its being broken up to be burnt for lime."

This colossal statue is recognised as an authentic portrait of Rameses II., "the celebrated conqueror, of the nineteenth dynasty." It was discovered, says Mariette, by Captain Caviglia, about the year 1820, and was presented to the British nation by Mehemet Ali. For three parts of the year it lies under water. There is reason to believe that it stood originally against the pylon of the Temple of Vulcan (Ptah), its face turned to the north; but of the temple itself not a vestige remains. According to custom, as evinced at Luxor and Karnak, there ought to have been another similar statue for the opposite side of the doorway, but we have searched for it in vain. Beyond the fact of correct portraiture it possesses no scientific value. According to Sharpe, the statue is forty-five feet in height.

Further on is Geezeh, with its magnificent group of pyramids, which are regarded, with much reason, as among the seven wonders of the world; and skirting the western bank of the river for, may be, fifty miles are other pyramids of inferior dimensions, amounting in the whole to close upon a hundred; one while in groups, as at Abooseer, Sakkarah, and Dashoor, another while in single file. The largest of the three great pyramids of Egypt was built by King Suphis, better known by the name of Cheops, as a resting-place for his embalmed body; the next in size was erected by his brother Susuphis or Chephren; and the third, which was cased in the red granite of Syené, is that of the son of Cheops—Menkara, also called Mycerinus. Besides these three, which are the *great** pyramids, there are six smaller ones in this group: and, fifteen miles further on, at the village of Sakkarah, is a pyramid

---

* The base of the great pyramid has been stated to be equal in size to the area of Lincoln's-Inn-Fields; but a "plan showing the comparative areas of the great pyramid and Lincoln's-Inn-Fields," drawn by Mr. Bonomi, of the Soane Museum, proves that this statement is correct only in respect of the long diameter of the square; for whilst one side of the base of the pyramid would extend westward from the wall of Lincoln's Inn (along the face of the houses on the *north* side of the square) to the middle of Gate Street, the southern boundary would overlap the buildings on the south side of the square, and take in the houses for some distance behind them, in the direction of the New Law Courts. A magnificent mausoleum! It is said that 100,000 men were employed for thirty years in its construction.

The Platform Pyramid. 53

built in steps, or platforms, which is said to be the oldest in the world;* older, by 500 or 700 years, than those of Cheops and Chephren; although these latter were erected 2,120 years before the birth of Christ, and, therefore, date back to a period of nearly 5,000 years.

A quarter of a mile to the south and east of the great pyramid is the colossal statue of the Sphynx, carved out of the summit of a rock, which crops up like an island in the midst of the sandy desert. The statue represents the couching body of a lion, with the head of a man, the union of power with intelligence, and is typical of royalty. The face, thirty feet in length by fourteen in breadth, has been much mutilated; its entire height is 100 feet, and its paws, which are fifty feet long, embrace a considerable area,

* Built by Ouenephes, the fourth king of the first dynasty. Mr. Bayle St. John says of it:—"This structure has a very peculiar form, and as it rises on its vast pedestal of rocky desert, seems totally distinct in character from all the other pyramids that break the horizon to the north and south. It has five steps only, five vast steps, that together rise to the height of nearly 300 feet. It looks like a citadel with a quintuple wall, five towers of gradually increasing elevation, one within the other."

having in its centre a sacrificial altar, and a space for religious worship. This huge memento of the past dates back to a period antecedent to the pyramids themselves, and marks the spot where two ancient

The Sphynx, with the great pyramid of Chafra, Susuphis or Chephren in the background.

temples formerly stood, one dedicated to Isis, the other to Osiris; both of which Cheops declares, on a tablet preserved in the museum at Boulak, were purified and restored by himself; whilst a neighbouring site was selected for the foundation of his own pyramid. The paws of the Sphynx are covered with inscriptions, among which is the following very interesting one, transcribed and translated by the distinguished Egyptologist, Dr. Thomas Young:—

"Thy form stupendous here the gods have placed,
Sparing each spot of harvest-bearing land;
And with this mighty work of art have graced
A rocky isle encumbered once with sand;
And near the pyramids have bid thee stand:
Not that fierce Sphynx that Thebes erewhile laid waste,
But great Latona's servant, mild and bland;
Watching that prince beloved who fills the throne
Of Egypt's plains, and calls the Nile his own:
That heavenly monarch (who his foes defies),
Like Vulcan powerful, and like Pallas wise."—*Arrian.*

"Even now," writes Dean Stanley, "after all that we have seen of colossal statues, there was something stupendous in the sight of that enormous head, * * * its vast projecting wig, its great ears, its open eyes, the red colour still visible on its cheek, the immense projection of the lower part of its face. Yet what must it have been when on its head there was the royal helmet of Egypt; on its chin the royal beard; when the stone pavement, by which men approached the pyramids, ran up between its paws; when, immediately under its breast an altar stood, from which the smoke went up into the gigantic nostrils of that nose now vanished from the face, never to be conceived again."*

On our left-hand, as we still stand gazing forward into the south, in the direction of the coming wavelets of the tawny Nile, is a desert plain, aforetime called the "Land of Goshen," lying between Cairo and the Suez Canal. It was here that Abraham found an abiding-place 1,920 years before the birth of Christ, when, driven out of Syria by the floods, he sought in Egypt herbage for his flocks and herds, and sustenance for his retainers. Here, in various stages of decay, are the ancient cities of the Hebrews, where Hebrew, until very recently, was the prevailing language of the people. Here we find On, or Onion, still bearing its Hebrew appellation, and Rameses and Pithom, and Succoth and Hieropolis. Nearer the Mediterranean Sea is "the field of Zoan" (Psalms, chap. lxxviii. ver. 12, 43), with the ruins of the ancient city of San, or

---

* "Sinai and Palestine in connection with their History." By Arthur Penrhyn Stanley, D.D., F.R.S.

Tanis, remarkable for the vast extent of the foundation of a once magnificent temple, teeming with monuments and obelisks. Here, says Mr. Macgregor, "you see about a dozen obelisks, all fallen, all broken; twenty or thirty great statues, all monoliths of porphyry and granite, red and grey." Isaiah had aforetime levelled his reproaches against San:—"The princes of Zoan are become fools, the princes of Nopth (Memphis) are deceived; they have also seduced Egypt, even they that are the stay of the tribes thereof." (Chap. xix. ver. 13.) And here was the gap through which the nations of Arabia, Syria, and Persia maintained intercourse with Egypt, one while as peaceful traders, another while as fugitives and outlaws, and again as enemies in arms. Here the shepherds or pastors made their predatory incursions, and conquered and subjected Lower Egypt; here the children of Israel began their exodus; and here, also, the Persians, the Greeks, and the Romans found an easy portal for their hostile invasion.

Eight miles away from Cairo, in the midst of a plot of sugar-cane, verdant with the luxuriance of its foliage, there stands forth against the sky a magnificent obelisk, the first that we have yet seen implanted on the spot where it was erected by its artificers. This obelisk bears the cartouche of Usertesen I.* (a Pharaoh of the twelfth dynasty, who ascended the throne 1,740 years before the Christian era), engraven on its face. It is not only the earliest and most ancient of all known obelisks, but it may be said to be the first page of the monumental history of Egypt: antecedent to it there is no record of monuments, save the pyramids and some ruined temples and tombs; but coeval with it, and illustrating the reign and acts of Usertesen, are the tombs of Beni Hassan, and

* In hieroglyphic writing the vowels are generally omitted, and a license is thereby given to insert them according to the taste or judgment of the translator: thus, if we assume the consonants s, r, ts, n, to represent a name, that name may be variously written, Usertesen, Ousertesen, Osertesen, Osirtasen, Osortasen, and so forth; and so much difference of opinion on this matter would seem to prevail among Egyptologists, that scarcely two can be found to precisely agree; and the same remark applies to other proper names:—for example, Thothmes, Thoutmes, Thothmosis; and Rameses, Ramses, Remeses, Ramisis, &c. Under these circumstances we have thought well to adopt the names sanctioned by the great British authority on Egyptology, Dr. Birch, of the British Museum.

the sanctuary, with its beautiful polygonal columns at Karnak, built by Usertesen himself.

The cartouches of Usertesen, as seen on the

The obelisk of Usertesen at Heliopolis, the most ancient obelisk in existence. In the background may be seen the Mokattan range of mountains, the barrier between the valley of Egypt and the Red Sea.

obelisk, represent his first and second names: the former, which implies divinity, consists of the sun's disk, a scarabæus, and a pair of human arms; and the oval is surmounted with two figures—a shoot of a plant and a bee, each supported on a hemisphere. These latter are royal titles, and imply the dominion of the king, or sun, over the south and the north, in addition to that part of the globe which is embraced by his own proper path, from east

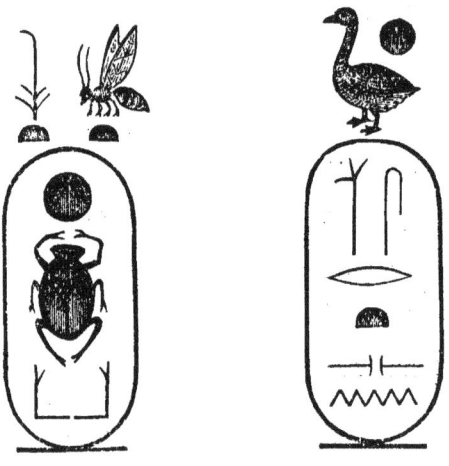

The Cartouches of Usertesen.

to west. The second oval contains the letters which constitute the word "Usertesen," and is surmounted by a disk representing the sun and a goose, the latter being the hieroglyph for "son," therefore, "son of the sun." So that the entire emblem may be supposed to read thus:—"The king; born and being of the sun; son of the sun; Usertesen."

On the spot occupied by this obelisk there

Temple of the Sun.

formerly stood a temple dedicated to the sun— to Ra, the rising sun; and to Toum or Tum, the setting sun. It is uncertain whether Usertesen founded the temple himself, or whether, as was the custom among the Pharaohs of Egypt, he simply contributed to its decoration and completion. But his name being sculptured on the face of the obelisk, serves to identify it with him. The temple of the sun was surrounded with habitations and temples of inferior mark, and became a city which, in their language, the Greeks named Heliopolis. Originally, there were two of these obelisks, as was lately corroborated by the discovery of the foundation of its fellow; but the shaft itself has long since disappeared, and nothing, save this one solitary obelisk, remains of the important city, in which Egyptians and Hebrews were united for many centuries in holy brotherhood. This monument, like the rest of the great obelisks of Egypt, was hewn in the quarries of rose-red granite of Syené. It is 67 feet 4 inches in height, and its pyramidion, now bare and without carving, was originally capped with gilt-bronze or some other metallic covering. Its hieroglyphs form a single central column, boldly and clearly carved, surmounted with the tutelar emblem and the standard of the king, and followed by the proper name and family name of Usertesen. The obelisk is stained for some distance up its shaft by the waters of the Nile, and, with its pedestal, is buried six or seven feet deep in the alluvium deposited by the stream.

While we credit Usertesen with these two obelisks, we have also to mention that portions of a broken shaft, engraven with hieroglyphs, which record his name, are to be met with at Biggig, in the Fyoom. These have been described as parts of a broken obelisk, but of an obelisk uncouth in its proportions, and terminated by a rounded point pierced with an opening as if for the purpose of receiving some ornament or finial. These characteristics of figure have led certain Egyptologists to treat of it as a monumental stone or tablet rather than as an obelisk, and the more so as it is situated on the western bank of the Nile; and supposing it to be an obelisk, is presumed to be the only monument of that kind met with on the western shore. A certain poetical hypothesis is also opposed to the belief; for the obelisk is the emblem of the *rising* sun and of life, and is therefore found only on the eastern bank of the Nile; whereas the western bank is presided over by the *setting* sun, and is therefore allied to the pyramids and tombs of the dead. The mounds of Memphis have not as yet been explored; but if an obelisk should be met with there at some future time, our dream of the privileges of the living and of the dead (already disturbed by Mariette's discovery of the pedestals of two obelisks, in front of the temple of Queen Hatasou, in Western Thebes), must share the fate of other pretty but illusory dreams. It seems hardly fair that the eastern bank should enjoy a monopoly of the sun's beaming rays, considering that tombs are also abundant along its rocky bounds.

But besides the ancient obelisks of Usertesen, there were four or more other obelisks at Heliopolis: two, which had received the name of Pharaoh's Needles, and were removed by Constantine—both of the period of Thothmes III.; and the two Thothmes-Rameses obelisks, or Cleopatra's Needles, which were set up at Alexandria.

When Napoleon, addressing his army in the desert of Libya, and pointing to the Pyramids, exclaimed, "Four thousand years look down upon you," his words had a deeper signification than the mere wakening up of a soldier's vanity. What, besides, have those Pyramids witnessed in that vast space of time? We now, in our turn, are called upon to ask the same question with reference to the obelisks of Heliopolis. The most ancient of those obelisks bears a date of seventeen centuries before the Christian era; not far short of the four thousand years of the Great Pyramids. The Thothmes obelisks date back about fourteen centuries before Christ, or more than three thousand years from the present time; and those of Rameses about twelve centuries, or 3,100 years.

The Heliopolis obelisk, it is true, was not erected until two hundred years after the arrival of Abraham in the land of Goshen; but it must have "looked down" on the caravan of Ishmaelite traders who brought Joseph a prisoner into Egypt, and sold him to Potiphar as a slave; on his sufferings and adventures in prison; on his skill in the interpretation of dreams; on his elevation to power by the Pharaoh of the day; and on that gratifying ceremony, when "Pharaoh called Joseph's name Zaphnath-paaneah," literally, revealer of secrets, "and when he gave him to wife Asenath, the daughter of Potipherah, priest of On." And no less does the obelisk point to that moment of filial devotion when "Joseph made ready his chariot, and went up to meet Israel his father, to Goshen; and presented himself unto him; and he fell on his neck, and wept on his neck a good while."

In the way from Cairo to Heliopolis, and near to the ruins of the latter, is a village called Matareeah, which has a similar signification to the word Heliopolis—namely, "town or place belonging to the sun." "Just before reaching the village of Matareeah, at a little distance from the road, on the right, is the garden in which is shown the sycamore tree,*

* This is called "The Virgin's Tree." The sycamore, or gimmis, bears a coarse kind of fig, and is therefore sometimes spoken of as a fig-tree. The trunk of the tree grows to the dimensions of twenty or thirty feet in diameter, and its wood is remarkable for its durability; hence it was used for the construction of mummy-cases, and also for that of gun-carriages and water-wheels.— McCoan.

beneath whose shade the Holy Family are said to have reposed after the flight into Egypt. It is a splendid old tree, still showing signs of life, but terribly mauled alike by the devout and the profane, who, respectively, have forgotten their piety and their scepticism in the egotistical eagerness to carry away and to leave a record of their visit. The present proprietor, a Copt, fearing lest their united efforts should result in the total disappearance and destruction of the tree, has put a fence round it, which, while it prevents the ruthless tearing off of twigs and branches, affords those who are anxious to commemorate their visit, a smooth and even surface, on which, with the help of a knife obligingly kept in readiness by the gardener, they may make their mark."*

We are now on the confines of the desert, where the air is reputed for its salubrity; and fifteen miles further on, at a distance of three miles from the river, Professor Flower takes notice of a warm sulphur spring, called Helwân, or Helouan des Bains, which has already been appropriated by invalids, and is

* Murray's Hand-book, 1875; p. 158.

Sulphur Springs of Helwân. 67

likely to become a rival of Aix-la-Chapelle, the baths of Switzerland, and those of the Pyrenees. Professor Flower informs us that a commodious bath establishment has been built on the spot, and has attracted the attention of numerous visitors. The temperature of the springs is 86° of Fahrenheit. A quarter of a century ago, Mr. Bayle St. John writes of Helwân as follows :—" We had resolved to visit the village of Helwân, parts of which we could just distinguish from our mooring-ground, peeping between groves of palms, sycamores, and acacias * * * with the bold line of rocks beyond. * * * The village, which has many neat houses, is approached on all sides between the lofty mud walls of gardens, full of trees, that, drooping over, form not unpicturesque avenues. An expanse of greensward, surrounded with sycamores, extends on one hand: altogether, the place is more agreeable to the eye than the generality of the Egyptian villages, principally on account of the great variety of foliage that nestles around it; for there are palms, and sycamores, and fig-trees and orange-trees, and locust-trees, and bananas and pomegranates. An immense number of doves cooed amorously in the branches."

The chronology of ancient Egypt is a subject not without its difficulties, open to a variety of opinion, and involved in perplexing uncertainty. Nevertheless, the mind naturally yearns for information as to the time of an occurrence, and the opportunity of comparing it with coincident events. Ptolemy Philadelphus made a first step towards a better state of knowledge, when in the year 250 B.C. he commissioned Manetho, an Egyptian priest, experienced in the learning of Heliopolis, to draw up a list of the kings of Egypt from the earliest times. Manetho performed his task ably; but, alas! the book was injured, and in troublous times a part of it was lost: nevertheless, that which remains is still a valuable record; and had the book been preserved entire, it would have settled many problems at present difficult of solution. Manetho groups the kings of Egypt into thirty-four reigning families or dynasties, each containing a number of kings, and by calculating backwards, from the known to the unknown, he arrives at the year 5504 B.C. as the date of

Menes, the first king of the first dynasty; that is to say, nearly seven thousand years from the present time. It is only fair to say, however, that several English authorities, including Sir Gardner Wilkinson, have declared against his dates, and have assumed the year 2700 B.C. to be more correct; Josephus says 2320; Bunsen, 3623; and Brugsch, 4455: in fact, a difference exists, on this point, between the German Egyptologists alone, of upwards of two thousand years. Under such circumstances it is encouraging to meet with an authority like Mariette Bey, Conservator of the Museum of Egyptian Antiquities at Boulak, one who has the best opportunities of investigation, and has devoted himself thoroughly to his work, express his confidence in the fidelity of Manetho's list, and, at least provisionally, adopt his dynasties and his dates. Modern discoveries, according to Mariette, have tended to corroborate Manetho's calculations; such, for example, as the tablets of Abydos, of which one is preserved in the British Museum, and more especially the tablet recently found by himself at Sakkarah, in the tomb of an Egyptian priest. Next we have the hieroglyphic evidence of the monuments, beginning with those of Usertesen; and later on, such further elucidation by the engraving on the monuments as serves to bring opposing opinion to an exact agreement. Thus, the date of the reign of Psammeticus I., of the twenty-sixth dynasty, as stated by Wilkinson, is 664 B.C.; while that of Bunsen and Mariette is 665 B.C.; even to a year.

All praise to the good old Egyptian priest, who wrote in Greek the chronology of his country's rulers; thanks to the industry and labour of Egyptologists, which have resulted in the corroboration of his researches; and thanks also to the Pharaohs who, in the midst of a splendid career of magnificence and victories, have found time for the meditations of the cloister, and have left behind them a consecrated attestation of the succession of their ancestors. In a small and secluded chapel adjoining the sanctuary of the great temple of Kàrnak, called the Hall of Ancestors, a record was found of Thothmes III. making oblations to sixty-one of his predecessors. This record is preserved in the national library of Paris; and whilst it verifies Manetho's list, is espe-

Succession of the Pharaohs. 71

cially correct as to the succession of the eighteenth dynasty, 1703 to 1464 B.C. The papyrus of Turin, so called from being preserved in that city, contains a list of the kings from the earliest period of Egyptian government, although the papyrus itself is broken into fragments. In the tablet of Abydos, preserved in the British Museum, Rameses II. does homage to fifty ancestors; but the names of twenty are lost. This tablet is a valuable record of the twelfth dynasty, 3064 to 2851 B.C., sustained by the family of Amenemha and Usertesen, and especially of the nineteenth dynasty, 1462 to 1288 B.C., the Ramessean period. A second tablet, similar to the above, and found in a companion temple, the one dedicated to Rameses II., the other to his father Seti, agrees in every respect with the British tablet. And last, though far from being the least, is the tablet of Sakkarah, found by Mariette in the tomb of an Egyptian priest, by name Tounar-i, of the time of Rameses II. The belief already existed in those days, that a well-behaved commoner, when he entered the land of spirits, might be permitted, as a reward of good conduct, to associate with kings; and so Tounar-i would seem to have prepared beforehand a list of his probable visiting acquaintance in the future world. Here he has assembled the cartouches of fifty-eight kings, closely corresponding with Manetho's list, and naturally with a respectful regard to precedency; so that his prospective visiting list admits of being turned to useful account by his successors. Saqqarah, or as it is commonly written, Sakkarah, is supposed to be the ancient Thinis, the capital of the Pharaohs of the first and second dynasties: the tablet is preserved in the museum at Boulak. On it we should doubtless find delineated the oval of Menes, with those of Cheops, Chephren, and Mycerinus, of the giant Apappus, and the rosy-cheeked but vengeful Nitocris.*

The pyramid and the obelisk have some-

* Apappus was a Pharaoh of gigantic build, and a successful general; he carried his wars into Ethiopia and Asia. He is said to have been nine feet high, and he lived to the age of 100 years.—The story of Queen Nitocris, the "belle with the rosy cheeks," as Manetho calls her, is, that her brother having been assassinated, she assembled together at a banquet all whom she thought to be accomplices in the crime; and when the hilarity of the evening was at its zenith, she let in upon them the waters of the Nile, so that they were all drowned.

thing analogous in their form—the four sides and the pointed summit—indeed, the apex of an obelisk, in nearly every case, is a diminutive pyramid, or pyramidion. Both had mystical attributes assigned to them in relation to the worship of the Sun, the "organiser of the world." The pyramid, with its four sides looking north, south, east, and west, was selected as the tomb of the mummified body which was destined to rise from the dead, and be restored to life at the appointed time. When the pyramid was too costly, a pair of small obelisks stood sentry at the entrance of the tomb, and were in common use during the early dynasties. A considerable number of these relics have been found, and preserved in the Egyptian museum at Boulak. The obelisk of Syenite granite, however, belongs to a later period; it may have come into use before the twelfth dynasty, before the reign of Usertesen; but the Heliopolis obelisk is generally admitted to be the pioneer of the colossal obelisks of the eighteenth and nineteenth dynasties, of the reigns of the Thothmeses and of the Ramseses. These latter were not funereal, but, on the contrary, were triumphal, and took the place of triumphal arches of modern times. On the facets of the pyramidion, and at the top of the shaft immediately below it, were usually engraved figures denoting supplication and gifts, by the Pharaoh who dedicates the monument, to the gods whom he intends to propitiate; it might be wine, or it might be milk; and occasionally, as at Heliopolis and at Karnak, the pyramidion was capped with metal, sometimes gold, from the countries which had been conquered in battle; sometimes burnished copper or bronze, which might represent the spoils of war, or by the reflection of its rays, an artificial sun; while certain of the obelisks are said to have been more extensively ornamented with metal.

We have ample evidence of the great care which has been bestowed on the preparation and finish of these Syenite obelisks: for example, the deep carving of the central column of hieroglyphs, and the shallow cutting of the side columns; the polish of the hollows of the hieroglyph to their extremest depth; and more strikingly still, in the gentle swell of the face of the shaft, intending to correct an error of reflection of light. This latter feature is especially noticeable in connection with the Luxor obelisks; and it has been observed, that but for this slight convexity, the surfaces of the column would have had the appearance of being concave.

The carvings of the obelisks usually began at the pyramidion occupying its lower half, and the inscriptions were engraven in narrow columns, each occupying one-third of the breadth of the shaft, the central column being the chief. Where the pyramidion was capped with metal, the engraving was absent on that part, as in the case of Usertesen's obelisk. In this obelisk we have also an example of a single column of inscriptions. In other instances, as in several of the Thothmes obelisks, and notably the British obelisk, the side spaces which were originally left blank, have been filled up by a successor of the founder, as in the case of Rameses II. The columns are to be read perpendicularly from top to bottom, and the base is sometimes decorated with symbols of thanksgiving. The inscriptions themselves were, for the most part, all of a similar character:—The Pharaoh approaches the deity with gifts, and on bended knee supplicates his blessing; this the deity vouchsafes; then, with floating banner, the standard of the king, the potentate recites his origin, his titles, and his deeds of usefulness and glory, rarely failing to include among them the raising of the obelisk; lastly, he finishes by a declaration of his power as a descendant of the sun, of giving life like his progenitor for everlasting.

Mr. W. R. Cooper, the Honorary Secretary of the Society of Biblical Archæology, has favoured us with the following translation of the hieroglyphs engraven on the British obelisk, extracted from Burton's "Excerpta Hieroglyphica." The illustration is, necessarily, limited to the three sides then exposed to view, and begins with the central column of each, containing the legend of Thothmes III.

First Side.—" The kingly Horus, strong bull, crowned in Thebes, the king of Upper and Lower Egypt, Ra-men-kheper; he made (this) in his monuments to his father, Horemakhou; he erected two very great obelisks, capped with gold, (when he celebrated) the panegyry of his father, who loves him. He did.

(it), the son of the sun, Thóthmes, the best of existences, beloved of Horemakhou."

Second Side.—" The kingly Horus, strong bull, ruling in truth, the king of Upper and Lower Egypt, Ra-men-kheper. For him the lord of gods has multiplied the panegyries (intervals of thirty years) in Habennou (the Temple of the Sun, in Heliopolis), knowing that he is his son, the elder, the divine flesh, issuing (from himself). The son of the sun, Thothmes, lord of Heliopolis, beloved of Horemakhou."

Third Side.—" The kingly Horus, strong bull, beloved of Ra (the sun), the king of Upper and Lower Egypt, Ra-men-kheper. His father Tum has established him, making for him a grandeur of name in expanded royalty .... in Heliopolis, (and) giving him the throne of Seb (and) the office of khepra; the son of the sun, Thothmes, the best of existences, beloved of the Bennou (sacred bird) of Heliopolis."

In the lateral columns, Rameses speaks as follows:—

First Side, 1.—" The kingly Horus, strong bull, son of Tum, the king of Upper and

Lower Egypt, Ra-ousor-ma-Sotep-en-Ra, lord of diadems, who protects Egypt and chastises nations; son of the sun, Ramessou Meriamen, who throws down southern peoples as far as the Indian Ocean, and the northern peoples as far as the prop of the sky; the lord of the two lands, Ra-ousor-ma-Sotep-en-Ra; son of the sun, Ramessou Meriamen, vivifier like the sun."

2.—"The kingly Horus, strong bull, beloved of Ma (truth), the king of Upper and Lower Egypt, Ra-ousor-ma-Sotep-en-Ra, lord of panegyries like his father, Ptah Totnen; son of the sun, Ramessou Meriamen, strong bull, like the son of Nou (Set); none could stand (against him) in his time, the lord of the two lands *(prenomen)*; son of the sun *(name)*."

Second Side, 1.—" The kingly Horus, strong bull, son of Khepra, the king of Upper and Lower Egypt *(prenomen)*. Golden hawk, of abundant years, very victorious; son of the sun *(name)*. (He) enabled men to behold (what) he has done; never was uttered denial (against it). The lord of the two lands *(prenomen)*; son of the sun *(name)*; splendour of the sun " . . . . . .

2.—" The kingly Horus, strong bull, beloved of Truth, the king of Upper and Lower Egypt *(prenomen)*; son of the sun, offspring of the gods, possessor of the two lands; son of the sun *(name)*, who made his frontiers to the place he chose, and got peace through his victory; the lord of the two lands *(prenomen)*; son of the sun *(name)*, splendour of the sun."

Third Side, 1.—" The kingly Horus, strong bull, beloved of Ra, the king of Upper and Lower Egypt *(prenomen)*; lord of panegyries, like his father, Ptah; son of the sun *(name)*; son of Tum, from his loins, who loves him; Hathor generated him; he who opened the two lands; lord of the two lands *(prenomen)*; son of the sun *(name)*, vivifier like the sun."

2.—" The kingly Horus, strong bull, son of . . . . . . the king of Upper and Lower Egypt *(prenomen)*; lord of diadems, who cares for Egypt and chastises nations; son of the sun *(name)*."

The Flaminian obelisk is a beautiful example of the species; it was constructed by the Pharaoh Seti I., otherwise Osirei, the blind king, or as he is designated by the carvings on the stone, Menephtha Sethai; and was completed by his son, Rameses II.: we therefore find his own personal narrative in the middle column, and that of the great Sesostris in the side columns. This obelisk was originally erected at Heliopolis, and was brought thence and conveyed to Rome by the Emperor Augustus in the tenth year before the Christian era. At Rome it was taken to the Circus Maximus or Campus Martius, where it would seem to have fallen into neglect, inasmuch as, at a later period, it was found partly buried and broken into three pieces. It was one of the five obelisks set up by Pope Sixtus V., and was placed by him in front of the church of St. Maria at the Porta del Popolo, the old Flaminian gate, in 1589; and although it has lost a portion of its base, is the third in height of the obelisks of Rome, measuring upwards of eighty-seven feet.

The Flaminian obelisk has been made the subject of an excellent paper, contributed to the Royal Society of Literature, in 1841, by the Rev. George Tomlinson, and published in the Transactions of the Society. Mr. Tomlinson produces a careful and exact translation of the inscription on all the sides of this obelisk; and as there is necessarily a considerable amount of repetition, we have endeavoured to curtail it, without, as we hope, doing injury to the sense. On three sides of the pyramidion Seti supplicates three separate deities:—Thoré of the sacred bark; Horus-phra, lord of the two worlds; and Athom, lord of Heliopolis. He appeals as follows:—" The good god, the Pharaoh, establisher of justice, the son of the sun, Menephtha-Sethai, says: Give me a life strong and pure. To which the deities reply: —We give thee all strength; we give thee a life strong and pure."

On the fourth side of the pyramidion, Rameses II., son of Seti, prefers a similar request to Athom, lord of Heliopolis, thus:— "The good god, the Pharaoh, guardian of justice, approved of the sun, the son of the sun, Ammon-mai Rameses, says: Give me a life strong and pure; and the deity responds:—We give thee a pure life."

At the top of the column, immediately under the pyramidion, is a square compartment, on which are sculptured figures of the king kneeling before the respective divinities, and

Standard of the King.

The subject of the woodcut is copied from the British obelisk, and represents the sacred hawk, the symbol of Horus, the deity of the Sun; surmounting the standard of the king, the Pharaoh, Thothmes III.

offering gifts, libations, vases of precious ointment, &c.

Next below the square compartment is another of oblong figure, divided into three stripes, corresponding with the three columns which descend the rest of the shaft down to its base. The upper part of the oblong space is occupied by the sacred hawk, capped with the helmet-shaped double crown of Egypt, and emblematical of the god Horus. Then follows the standard of the king in the form of a banner representing a bull, the emblem of power and moderation, together with the special attributes of the king. The inscription in the oblong compartment will therefore read as follows:—The Horus, the powerful; then, in the case of Seti; sanctified by truth and justice; the piercer of foreign countries by his victories; the beloved of the sun and justice. Whilst the legend of Rameses styles him:—The beloved of the sun; the son of Noubti or Seth; the beloved of justice; the son of Ptha Totonen; and the son of Athom.

The vertical columns commemorative of Seti are as follows:—The Horus, the powerful, sanctified by truth and justice, &c. Lord of the diadems of Upper and Lower Egypt, Month or Mandou of the world; possessor of Egypt; the resplendent Horus, the Osiris, the divine priest of Thoré; the king, Pharaoh, establisher of justice, who renders illustrious the everlasting edifices of Heliopolis, by foundations fit for the support of the heaven; who has established, honoured, and adorned the Temple of the Sun and the rest of the gods; which has been sanctified by him, the son of the sun, Menephtha-Sethai, the beloved of the spirits of Heliopolis, everlasting like the sun.

The variations in other columns speak of Seti as "the establisher of everlasting edifices, making his sanctuary in the sun, who loves him, the adorner of Heliopolis, who makes libations to the sun and the rest of the lords of the heavenly world, who gives delight by his rejoicings and by his eyes: beloved of Horus, the lord of the two worlds:"—"The scourge of foreign countries, piercer of the shepherds, who fills Heliopolis with obelisks to illumine with their rays the Temple of the Sun; who like the Phœnix fills with good things the great temple of the gods, causing it to overflow with rejoicing."

The vertical columns in praise of Rameses proclaim as follows:—" The Horus, the powerful, the beloved of the sun, the Ra, the offspring of the gods, the subjugator of the world, the king, the Pharaoh, guardian of justice, approved of the sun; son of the sun, Ammon-mai Rameses; who gives joy to the region of Heliopolis when it beholds the radiance of the solar mountain. He who does this is lord of the world; the Pharaoh, guardian of justice, approved of the sun, son of the sun, Ammon-mai Rameses, giving life like the sun."

In another column he calls himself:—" The beloved of justice, who has erected edifices like the stars of heaven; he hath made his deeds resound above heaven, scattering the rays of the sun, rejoicing over them in his house * * * In the * * year of his majesty he made good this edifice of his father, whom he loved, giving stability to his name in the abode of the sun. He who hath done this is the son of the sun, Ammon-mai Rameses, the beloved of Athom, lord of Heliopolis, giving life for ever."

In a third column he is called " The director of the years, the great one of victories." In a fourth:—" The Ra, begotten of the gods, the subjugator of the world, who magnifies his name in every region by the greatness of his victories." Again:—he is termed " The lord of panegyries,* like his father Ptha-Totonen, begotten and educated by the gods, builder of their temples, lord of the world; a son of Thoré."

At the base of the obelisk, on the north side, Seti kneels before the hawk-headed deity Hor-phra, Horus, or the Sun, offering gifts: the god says:—" The speech of Hor-phra, lord of the two worlds. We give thee vigour, magnanimity, and strength, to have a life pure, and like the sun, everlasting."

On the south side he says:—" The speech

* Sir Gardner Wilkinson writes:—"Of the fixed festivals, one of the most remarkable was the celebration of the grand assemblies, or panegyries, held in the great halls of the principal temples, at which the king presided in person. That they were of the greatest importance is abundantly proved by the frequent mention of them in the sculptures; and that the post of president of the assemblies was the highest possible honour, may be inferred as well from its being enjoyed by the sovereign alone, of all men, as from its being assigned to the deity himself in these legends:—' Phra (Pharaoh), lord of the panegyries, like Re,' or, 'like his father Ptha.' "

of Hor-phra, the enlightener of the two worlds, the great god, the lord of heaven: we give thee all the worlds, all the countries * * * and to be lord of the south and the north, like the sun, sitting for ever upon the throne of Horus."

On the east side of the base of the obelisk Rameses kneels before Athom (the setting sun), and offers, with his left hand, one of the pyramidal cakes common in Egypt. The deity says—" We, Athom, lord of Heliopolis, the great god, give thee the throne of Seb (Saturn), the altar of Athom * * * the diadems of Horus and Noubti, in a pure life."

As another example of the inscriptions on obelisks, we quote a translation of the middle column of the west face of the Paris obelisk, as follows:—" The sun Horus, with the strength of the bull, lover of Truth, sovereign of the north and south, protector of Egypt, and subjugator of the foreigner, the golden Horus, full of years, powerful in the fortress, King Ra-user-ma, chief of chiefs, was begotten by Toum, of his own flesh, by him alone, to become King of the Earth, for ever and ever, and to supply with offerings the temple of Ammon.

"It is the son of the sun, Ramses-meri-Amon, eternally living, who constructed this obelisk."

It may be as well to explain, that the sun being deified by the Egyptians as the symbol of creation, the maker, the disposer; and the Pharaohs being supposed to be sons of the sun, the rising sun Ra, being generated out of Toum, or Tum, the setting sun; the rising sun, therefore, becomes, at one and the same time, both father and son.

One of the inscriptions on Cleopatra's Needle at Alexandria is as follows:—

"The glorious hero, the mighty warrior, whose actions are great on the banner; the king of an obedient people; a man just and virtuous, beloved by the Almighty Director of the universe; he who conquered all his enemies, created happiness throughout all his dominions, who subdued his adversaries under his sandals.

"During his life he established meetings of wise and virtuous men, in order to introduce happiness and prosperity throughout his empire. His descendants, equal to him in glory and power, followed his example. He was, therefore, exalted by the Almighty-seeing Director of the world. He was the lord of Upper and Lower Egypt; a man most righteous and virtuous, beloved by the All-seeing Director of the world."

The Thothmes-Rameses obelisks, subsequently called Cleopatra's Needles; and one of them, now, the British obelisk, were erected by Thothmes III., in front of the portico of the great temple of Heliopolis; where Moses pursued his studies and became skilled in Egyptian learning, and where he afterwards filled the office of professor or priest. Many, many times, no doubt, must Moses have contemplated the pagan proclamations on these obelisks, and have contrasted them, in his own mind, with the simple language of the living God Most High, whom he himself worshipped. Many times he must have shuddered at the pagan oppression of his own people, and felt himself appealed to for their protection. Who shall say that the immolation of the Egyptian who was discovered striking a Hebrew was not a righteous act. Cruelties had been suffered by the

Israelites until they could be borne no longer, and this blow from the hand of an Egyptian became the starting-point of the future exodus. Many years later Moses proved his capacity as a leader,* and conducted his brethren safely across the Red Sea, pursued by Menephtah III., the Pharaoh of the day, the son and successor of that Rameses whose oval is impressed on the British obelisk. The date of Joseph's advent in Egypt has latterly been referred to the period of the shepherd kings, who are supposed to have been of Jewish descent, and therefore more likely to be disposed favourably towards Joseph than the Egyptian Pharaohs. The dynasties of the shepherd kings ranged between 2214 and 1703 B.C.

A little fusillade of guns reminds us that the time has arrived when we must bid farewell to the Queen of Eastern cities, and embark on the enchanting Nile for the ancient city of Thebes, just 450 miles away. A shriek from the railway train on the west bank suggests that we may shorten our pilgrimage by nearly

* Moses is said to have been eighty years old at the time of the exodus.

200 miles; a well-known pant from the river tells us that a steam-boat is at hand, destined to carry passengers and scare crocodiles* in its journey to the first cataract. But we have dreamed of a Nile voyage in the graceful Nile boat, the "Dahabeeyah," with its huge lateen sail, for many and many a month; we have enjoyed, by anticipation, the quiet, the repose, and the opportunity for contemplation which the voyage of the Nile for several weeks† must afford, and our mind has long since been made up; the guns again fire their parting salute, the anchor is tripped, and we spring away from our moorings like a bird

* It is a curious fact that the crocodile is rarely met with now, even in Upper Egypt, but requires to be sought after higher up the river—namely, in Nubia. It is said to be a timid creature, and the steam-boat and rifle have scared it from its ancient haunts. Mr. A. C. Smith, who is a zealous ornithologist, identifies the bird that ventures into the mouth of the crocodile in search of leeches—the crocodile bird—as the spur-winged plover (charadrius spinosus), the Zic-Zac of the Arabs, which has constituted itself the professional toothpicker of the crocodile.

† Professor Flower mentions that the voyage from Cairo and back occupies from eight to ten weeks; while that to and from the second cataract requires a month longer.

enjoying its first flight on a summer's morning. Upon either side of the river-stream is the narrow strip of arable earth, green with its luxuriant crops, so peculiar to the land of Egypt; beyond are the yellow sands of the desert; and further off, constituting the frame in which the picture is set, is the range of orange-red sandstone rocks, which shuts in the valley of the Nile on both its sides. As we move onwards we seem to be reviewing a section of the earth—the alluvium of the Delta behind us; the sandstone, the gritstone, the limestone of the secondary rocks, rising into a wall on either side, with the porphyry, the syenite, and the granite of the primary rock awaiting us at the first cataract, the gates of Egypt. The rocks approach nearer to the river as we advance, and keep us company to the end of our journey; sometimes they are so close as to stand up like perpendicular cliffs, and encroach on the tawny stream; and at other times they recede, and encircle an extensive valley, such as that on which the grandest ruins in the world, those of the ancient city of Thebes, are heaped up. This rock-bound valley is bisected by the

Nile: on the one side, the west, are the ruins of once magnificent temples and royal tombs; on the other, the east, the up-piled heaps of gigantic *débris;* the Nile dividing the abodes of the living from those of the dead. On the west side are temples dedicated to Rameses I. by his son Seti I.; to Seti I. by Rameses II.; and to Rameses II. by Rameses himself; a temple to Queen Hatasou, and temples to Amenophis III. and Rameses III. Then we have valleys enshrined with tombs of kings and queens, dating from Seti I. downwards to Rameses IV. In the tomb of Seti, Belzoni secured the beautiful sarcophagus of white alabaster, one of the choice relics deposited in the Soane Museum; and from the tomb of Rameses III., discovered by Bruce, was obtained the sarcophagus of red granite, the cyst of which is preserved in the Louvre, and the covercle, or lid, in the Fitzwilliam Museum at Cambridge; whilst round and about are necropolises of considerable extent, for the most part appendages of the temples.

Once upon a time there existed on this spot a temple of calcareous stone; the temple was named Memnonium, from being situated in a part of the city called Memnonia; and the trumpet of fame has ascribed it to a mythical king, Memnon: it was, however, erected by Amenophis or Amunoph III., who, for no

The Memnonian Colossi; one of the two being the "Vocal Memnon." They are sitting statues of the Pharaoh, Amenophis III.

better reason, has likewise been termed Memnon. Egyptologists deplore the loss of this temple, as it no doubt contained the historical record of the reign of Amenophis; but of its pylons, its walls, and its columns, nothing now remains save their foundations; its stones have been broken into bits, and the bits have been carried away and burnt into lime. Nevertheless, a memorial of its former existence happily remains in the two gigantic colossal statues of Amenophis, which were carved out of breccia, a transition rock, that could yield no lime by the burning. These are the two huge Colossi, still grand, but much defaced and injured, which sat at their ease in front of the pylon of Amunoph's temple, and will sit on, perhaps, for centuries, although the sanctuary which they once guarded and adorned is no more. Of another temple near at hand, M. Mariette says:—"The lime-burners have luckily not yet found their way here. But why? Simply because there is already so much limestone among the ruins on the plain, which is, therefore, more easy of acquisition;" but when this shall have been exhausted, then looms another invasion of those industrious shepherds, the lime-burners.

No doubt, a good deal of the destruction which we see around was the handiwork of man, perhaps of the baffled Cambyses; perhaps of Ptolemy Lathyrus, those two great destroyers; but history reminds us, that in the twenty-seventh year before the birth of Christ, an earthquake visited Egypt, and shook it to its very foundations. This earthquake seriously damaged the Colossi, and more especially the northernmost one, which had its upper part shaken completely off. But a curious phenomenon succeeded. Of a morning, when the sun first rose and warmed the statue, it gave forth a plaintive wail, resembling the sound of the human voice. This, apparently, resulted from some contraction or expansion of the material of the broken stump: it has been supposed that the fractured stone, moistened by the dew of night, crackled under the drying influence of the warm rays of the rising sun. But whatever the physical cause may have been, the sound attracted the notice of travellers; and visitors came from all parts of the surrounding countries to witness the phenomenon. It would seem that the event was a little fickle; it did not always manifest itself, nor precisely at the same time; but it was only at or about the time of the rising of the sun that it was evoked. To the multitude, this sound was the voice of Memnon lamenting to his divine mother, Aurora, the injuries his statue had sustained; and in this wise he sighed forth his lament for 250 years, when Septimus Severus stretched forth his hand to heal his wounds, and perchance to elicit a happier, cheerfuller note. The statue was repaired by means of blocks of stone, as in ordinary masonry; the voice of lamentation ceased, and with it every vestige of sound. Memnon wailed and sighed no more, neither did his voice come more melodiously forth as his restorer hoped. The vocal Memnon sunk at once, from an object of wonder, to the simple rank of the northern colossus of Amenophis. But the term Colossus is well earned when we reflect that the statue itself was fifty feet in height; while its pedestal of ten feet gave it an altitude of sixty feet. Two figures standing against the arms of the throne on which the giant sits, are those of his mother and sister.

Not far away from the ruin of the Memnonium and the Memnonian Colossi are the fragments of a temple, erected by Rameses II., and dedicated to himself, the Ramesseum; it has likewise been named the Palace of Memnon and the Tomb of Osymandias. But the object of chief interest for us, at the present time, in connection with this ruin, is the broken Colossus, which formerly stood within the entrance-court of the temple. The statue is wrought out of Syenite granite; it was brought from Syené, and is one of the most gigantic monoliths carved by the Egyptians. It is a statue of Rameses the Great, seated on his throne, in the attitude of repose, and was originally nearly forty feet high; whilst its estimated weight was very little short of 900 tons. It is now broken across at the waist; the lower part is shattered into fragments; whilst the upper portion is reduced in size by the cutting out of mill-stones by the Arabs. "It is difficult," says Mariette, "at what most to wonder, the patience and labour of the sculptor, or the pains and force employed by the destroyer." Miss Edwards, speaking of this Colossus, remarks, that "the stone is so hard, that when small fragments are mounted on a handle, they are used as a substitute for the diamond by engravers of antiques."

But we must confess to a little, a very little, malice when we turn the attention of our readers to Deir-el-Bahari, a temple erected to the honour of Hatasou, also on the western and sepulchral side of Thebes. "Here," says Mariette, "we find a temple mounting the rock behind it by regular steps or platforms, and built of a beautiful white and marble-like calcareous stone. It was formerly approached by a long avenue of sphinxes, and heralded by *two obelisks*, of which the bases alone are now traceable."

But how, may we venture to enquire, came obelisks, the offspring of the rising sun, on the Hades side of the Nile? Can the river have changed its course? Alas! no. It is the whim of woman. Hatasou erected the grandest obelisks in existence; she covered the whole shaft, with the exception of the carvings, with gold. She erected a temple that stepped up the side of a mountain, as if it were a flight of stairs. She governed Egypt, the two worlds, and maintained the dignity of the diadems of the upper and lower country during one of the most brilliant periods of Egypt's greatness; and now we find her imparting sunshine to the dead, and by exception proving the rule, that no obelisks are to be found on the western bank of the Nile, saving her own, and the flouted fragments of Fyoom. "She hath made this work for her father Amun-re, lord of the regions; she hath erected to him this handsome gateway * * * Amun protects the work * * * she hath done this to whom life is given for ever."* So says the Pharaoh Amun-noo-het, or Hatasou. Turn we now to the eastern bank of the Nile, and we find the Arab village of Luxor grown up like a parasitic fungus over the ruins of once stately edifices, the grand temple of Amenophis III., where the Colossi of Rameses guard the entrance; and two miles away, the still more magnificent ruin of the temple of Usertesen and his successors: but of these anon.

The inscription on the paw of the sphynx, already noted, has reminded us how precious to the Egyptian is every "spot of harvest-bearing land," so precious that not a tittle could be spared for the interment of the dead; the sands were too shifting, and the sandstone rock alone remained for the purposes of burial. The sandstone rock forms a broad shelf at the border of the desert, and thence mounts up in terraces to the summit of the mountain-range.

* Murray.

Cheops and Chephren, and the kings of the early dynasties, had the power and the means of raising mountains over their embalmed and mummified remains; but for the people, must suffice a more humble resting-place;—for them a hole was scooped out on the platform of rock, to be built up at its entrance until the day of resurrection should arrive. In the neighbourhood of the Pyramids, the cemetery of kings, the sandstone rock is honeycombed with tombs, in which the population of every degree have their appropriate sepulchral niche. In later times these tombs have been ransacked for antiquarian relics and for the riches they contained;, and the desert around is still thickly carpeted with a profuse accumulation of fragments of mummies and mummy-cases, and vestments of every kind.

The word mummy is said to be derived from "moum," a kind of wax used in the process of embalming. This process would seem to have been first employed during the eleventh dynasty, about 3,000 years before the Christian era, and to have been practised until the 6th century A.D. Mariette notes differences in the appearance and qualities of the mummies in accordance with their source—from Memphis or Thebes, or their preparation in more recent times. The Memphite mummies are extremely dry, break easily, and are black in colour; those of Thebes are tightly bandaged, yellow and flexible, bending easily, and sometimes preserving so much softness as to admit of being indented by pressure: whereas, in later times, the bodies were saturated with a kind of turpentine from Judea, and became heavy, compact, the bandages seemingly identified with the flesh, and so hard as only to be broken with violence. The Memphite mummies were often filled with amulets and scarabæi, and by their sides, or between their legs, was placed a papyrus, a copy of the Book of the Dead. On the Theban mummies were scarabæi and rings, which were worn on the fingers of the left hand.

The essentials of a tomb, for such as could afford the expense, were, a deep quadrangular well in the rock; in the side of this well was a smaller cavity for the deposit of the mummy, or of the mummy-case; after which, the entrance of the cavity, or grave, was carefully walled up; next followed a chamber in which mourners and friends could assemble; and after that a portal, or exterior entrance, by which admission might be obtained. It is easy to understand how this simple design may be amplified until an entire rock of considerable magnitude has been hollowed out into numerous chambers; how these chambers may be ornamented with columns and sculptures; how the portal may assume an architectural form, and become a pylon, and the front of the rock be

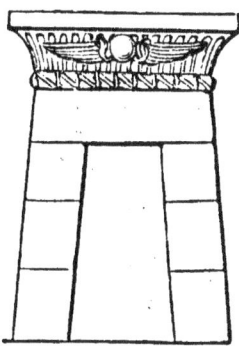

A pylon or doorway of a house or temple.

carved into columns and statues of imposing grandeur and beauty. Indeed, there would seem—as in fact is the case—no bounds to the intricacy and extent of the sanctuary and its chambers, the elegance and decoration of the appurtenant halls, and the magnificence and grandeur of the pylonic front. We should be pleased to imagine that the first efforts of man practised on the rocks, and thence transferred to the plain, were the early origin of Egyptian architecture, were we not aware of the fact, that the work of the mason makes its appearance seemingly contemporaneously with that of the wonderful excavations, of which so many examples are to be met with on the banks of the Nile.

Arrived at Thebes, we find the rock and tomb architecture especially illustrated on the western bank of the Nile; while the masonic element appears in all its grandeur on the eastern bank, in the temples of Karnak and Luxor, magnificent in the midst of overwhelming ruin. At Karnak, the foundation of the principal temple is a mile and a-half in circuit: it was founded by Usertesen, of the twelfth dynasty, and has been enlarged by successive additions of courts and halls, by Thothmes I. and his family, by Seti I. and Rameses II. and their family, and subsequently by a long series of kings, ending with Alexander the Greek.

One of the most interesting features of these

Propylon of Edfoo.

magnificent temples is the doorway, or *pylon*, which, from the simplest form, ornamented in the simplest manner, and serving as the humble entrance of the cavern in the rock, has become developed into an architectural structure of surpassing grandeur and importance. When it stands independently, in advance of the proper entrance of the temple, it is termed *propylon;* and the propylon is often a

The propylon, or tower-gate, of the temple of Edfoo, one of the most magnificent in Egypt. Its breadth is 250 feet, and height 115. The temple itself, which is one of the most perfect specimens of Egyptian temple-architecture, was founded by Ptolemy Philopater, and the propylon was erected by Ptolemy Dyonysus. The entire structure is Ptolemaic, and it is ornamented on every side with paintings and sculptures. The small buildings at its base are the houses of the village.

massive structure, which resembles a tower or a fortress rather than a simple gate or portal. It consists usually of a thick wall, pyramidal in its figure, of considerable height, and terminated above by a broad cornice ornamented over the portal with the winged orb, the type of the Eternal and of the sun; the centre of the wall being perforated by the doorway, or entrance. The propylon is generally furnished with two flag-staves fixed to its front, and sometimes divides at the top into a pair of towers.* As the propylon is the representative of the ornamented entrance of the temple, the *fore*-gate, or *fore*-tower, it is a necessary appurtenance to the temple, and

---

* Miss Edwards remarks, that there is preserved in the Egyptian room of the Glyptothek Museum at Munich, a statue of the chief architect of the Ramessian period, Bak-en-khonzu, who, "having obtained the dignity of High Priest and First Prophet of Ammon, during the reign of Seti I., became chief architect of the Thebaid under Rameses II., and received a royal commission to superintend the embellishment of the temples. When Rameses II. erected a monument to his divine father Ammon-Re," Bak-en-khonzu "made the sacred edifice in the upper gate of the abode of Ammon. He erected obelisks of granite. He made golden flag-staffs. He added very, very great colonnades."

forms a picturesque object when seen from a distance; whilst its walls are made subservient to the purposes of painting and sculpture, destined to illustrate the history of its founder. The propylon of the most modern portion of the temple at Karnak is 140 feet high, 370 feet in breadth, and 50 feet in thickness; it is approached by an avenue of ram-headed sphynxes, 200 feet long, and the sides of the doorway were formerly ornamented with two granite statues, which are now in a state of ruin.

The peculiar characteristics of ancient Egyptian architecture are, its obelisks, its pylons or propylons, its colossal statues, and its superb columns. At the entrance of the temple at Karnak, leading into the Hall of Rameses II., we have the colossal sphynxes and statues and propylon, and passing through the latter we enter a spacious hall decorated with superb columns. At the end of this hall we approach another propylon, its doorway supported on either side by a statue of Rameses III.; and this gives entrance to the great Hall of Seti I. and Amenophis III., enriched with 134 columns, and said to be the largest and most magnificent of ancient Egyptian monuments. Beyond the great hall are a third and a fourth propylon, and between them an obelisk, one of a pair erected by Thothmes I. The obelisk is seventy-five feet high, and is covered on one face with hieroglyphs descriptive of its founder, while the opposite face is occupied with sculptured writing of Rameses II. For the second time we are made aware of this remarkable combination—shall we call it appropriation?—by Rameses. The brother-obelisk has fallen, and is broken into fragments.

Through the entrance of the fourth propylon we are admitted into a hall ornamented with columns whose capitals represent the head of Osiris. This is the Hall of Thothmes I.; and by the side of its doorway stands another obelisk, 92 feet in height, and 8 feet square at the base. There were originally two of these splendid obelisks; but its consort is fallen, and has been dashed into bits. These are the obelisks that bear the legend on their base of having been hewn from the rock, and erected in the short space of seven months; of having been capped with gold taken from the enemies of the country, and of being emblazoned with gold-leaf from bottom to top: they were set up by Hatasou, daughter of Thothmes I., in honour of her father. Hatasou was her father's favourite; he, no doubt, discovered in her, indications of talent fitting her for the throne, and he appointed her his successor. In this capacity she became the guardian of her brother, Thothmes II., who died at an early age; and, subsequently, of the distinguished potentate, her brother, Thothmes III., who was not admitted to the throne for fifteen years after the death of his brother. Many grand works in architecture owe their origin to Queen Hatasou, and to these her cartouche was affixed; but, in later times, she was treated as an usurper; her name was erased from the monuments, and that of her brother substituted in its place.

Beyond the Hall of Osiris we reach the original temple and sanctuary containing the tomb and funereal chambers founded by Usertesen; and further on still, and forming the end of the pile, a temple erected by Thothmes III. Here, therefore, we observe a striking illustration of the combination of many potentates in the construction of these wonderful examples of architectural skill. The first stone of this temple was laid, probably, 3064 B.C., and the building was scarcely completed in the year 1288 B.C.; a period embracing 1,776, or nearly 2,000 years, being devoted to its construction.

In the neighbourhood of the great temple of Karnak are the ruins of a smaller temple appertaining to Amenophis III. "It was once adorned with elegant sculptures and two granite obelisks; but is now a confused heap of ruins, whose plan is with difficulty traced beneath its fallen walls."* Of course, the obelisks are lost. The Temple of Luxor likewise owes its origin to Amenophis III.; and was extended, a century and a-half later, by Rameses II.; the latter monarch adding a magnificent hall, a propylon of vast dimensions, two colossal sitting statues of himself, a pair of beautiful obelisks, and an avenue of sphynxes nearly two miles in length, stretching away from Luxor to Karnak. Approaching the temple by the avenue of sphynxes, about 500 in number, we meet with the now solitary obelisk,

* Murray's "Hand-book."

The Luxor Obelisks.

its consort having been removed to Paris; next comes the majestic propylon, its entrance guarded by two helmeted colossal sitting

Plan of ornamentation of the entrance of an Egyptian temple—*e.g.*, that of Luxor. In front and on either side of the pylon are the obelisks. Nearer the jambs of the pylon are two colossal sitting statues of Rameses II., wearing the double crown of Egypt; then follows the pylon itself, with its two majestic pyramidal towers. The pylon is surmounted with an over-hanging cornice, on which is carved the winged orb, emblem of the Eternal and of the sun; while two crowned asps, one on each side of the disk, imply dominion over the north and the south, as well as the east and the west; consequently over the whole world.

statues of Rameses II., carved out of black granite, and half buried in the earth. Passing the portal, we enter the great Hall of Rameses, and, beyond that, reach the sanctuary of Amenophis. The obelisk bears the name of Rameses, and is remarkable for the beauty and depth of its carving—a circumstance which may possibly have influenced the French in their selection. Sir Gardner Wilkinson made a curious discovery with regard to the Paris obelisk, which he narrates as follows:—

"Being at Luxor when it was taken down, I observed beneath the lower end on which it stood the nomen and pre-nomen of Rameses II., and a slight fissure extending some distance up it; and what is very remarkable, the obelisk was cracked previous to its erection, and was secured by two wooden dove-tailed cramps. These, however, were destroyed by the moisture of the ground, in which the base had become accidentally buried."

The hieroglyphs on its face, announce that "the lord of the world, guardian-sun of truth, approved of Phra; has built this edifice in honour of his father, Ammon-Ra, and has erected to him these two great obelisks of stone, in face of the House of Rameses, in the city of Ammon."*

* Miss Edwards.

Besides the Luxor obelisks, numerous others are ascribed to Rameses II.—namely, the two small monoliths at Rome, one in the Piazza Rotunda in front of the Pantheon, the other at the Villa Mattei; as also the ten broken obelisks at San, on the field of Zoan: while two more bear the joint names of his father Seti and himself; for example, the beautiful column of the Piazza del Popolo, known as the Flaminian Obelisk, and that of the Trinita de Monti at Rome.

It is a curious fact in connexion with the history of obelisks, that two of the most stately—indeed, the next in height to that of St. John Lateran—should have been the work of a woman, Queen Hatasou, daughter of Thothmes I., and guardian for a while of Thothmes III. But when the reins of power fell into the hands of the latter, he seems to have treated his sister as an usurper, and to have obliterated her name from the monuments, while he substituted in its place the cartouche of his own; so that the work of Hatasou is usually ascribed to Thothmes III. We find a similar illustration in the relation between Rameses II. and his father, Seti I.

Seti was distinguished in his early life as a warrior, but, unfortunately, was stricken with blindness; he thereupon resigned the throne to his son, and retired into solitude. By degrees he recovered his sight, and devoted the rest of his life to architecture and building. His cartouche is to be found amongst the magnificent ruins at Thebes; and he was the author of several obelisks: in the latter instance his name is associated with, and occasionally replaced by, that of his son. The son of the blind man, the great Sesostris, Rameses II., must be supposed to have encouraged this substitution, for he has obtained credit for much that was not really his own; and to such an extent has misconception been carried, that Rameses and Seti have been identified as one and the same person; while a younger son of Rameses, Menephtah, has been described as the son of the king who went blind. Another element of confusion is the Greek name—Sesostris, given to Rameses II. Rameses was celebrated as a victorious soldier; as also was his distinguished predecessor, Thothmes III. Sesostris is described by Herodotus as a great conqueror;

and as this character applies equally to Thothmes and Rameses, these two kings, although 200 years apart in point of time, become awkwardly confounded with each other. It would be ungenerous to suppose that such a state of confusion was acceptable to Rameses and favoured his designs; or that it could have led him to adopt that association with the memory of Thothmes which is implied by the sculptures on the Thothmic obelisks: although it must be admitted that there certainly exist grounds for the suspicion. In this respect Rameses would almost seem to have been the victim of an idiosyncrasy. In fact, Rameses II. is accused of monopolising the reputation of all the great deeds enacted during more than 600 years, from the time of Thothmes II. to that of Shishonk, or, as he is named in the Bible, Shishak, the conqueror of Jerusalem.

We have compared the village of Luxor to a crop of mushrooms overgrowing a mountain of architectural ruins; and so it would seem to be: the mud huts of the Arabs and Copts at first sheltered themselves under the massive walls, then crept up to the cornices and roofs,

Sacred Scarabæi.

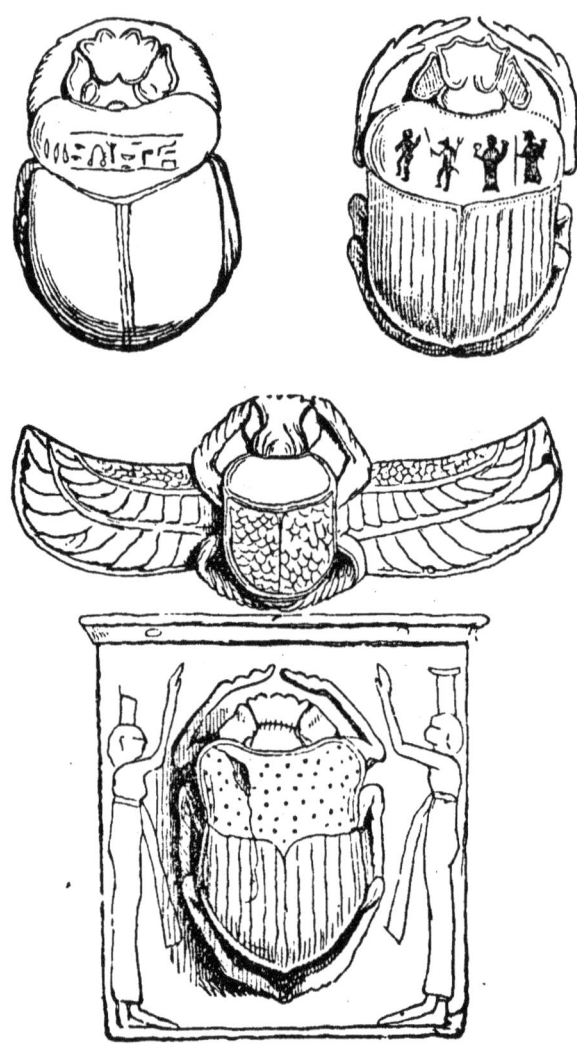

Sacred scarabæi, or beetles. On the back of the thorax of the upper pair are engraven mythological figures and hieroglyphics; the middle scarab is furnished with wings like the winged orb; the lower one has human supporters. The scarabæus is the emblem of future being, or future existence, and is often introduced into the body of the mummy to take the place of the heart, which is embalmed separately. The four figures probably represent the four keepers to whom the heart is confided, and the hieroglyphics are verses from the Book of the Dead.

and in time, like swallows' nests, stuccoed every hollow and niche where sufficient space could be obtained for a resting-place. Only that they were forbidden, they would have occupied the whole of the temples and their halls, hypostyle and hypæthral, and have left nothing visible but themselves. The inhabitants of these huts are poor and ragged; but, according to Lady Duff Gordon (who lived amongst them for a long time, and between whom and them a warm attachment subsisted, fostered by her own humanity and kindness), they are remarkable for cleanliness, both in their persons and in their huts. Luxor, however, is the great emporium of antiques, and an active manufacture of scarabæi or sacred beetles, of statuettes, and even of tablets, is carried on by the Arab traders. "It is the centre," says M. Mariette, "of a commerce more or less legal, inasmuch as the rummaging of tombs is now prohibited by law. Nevertheless, it requires much judgment, and often that of the expert, to distinguish with certainty between the genuine and the fictitious." Miss Edwards relates that she was once accidentally ushered

118   *Scarabs and Amulets.*

into the workshop of a dealer, where she saw tools and appliances in number for the fabrication of these objects, so eagerly sought after by the traveller. On the arrival of the proprietor she was speedily shown out, but overheard the scoldings which were

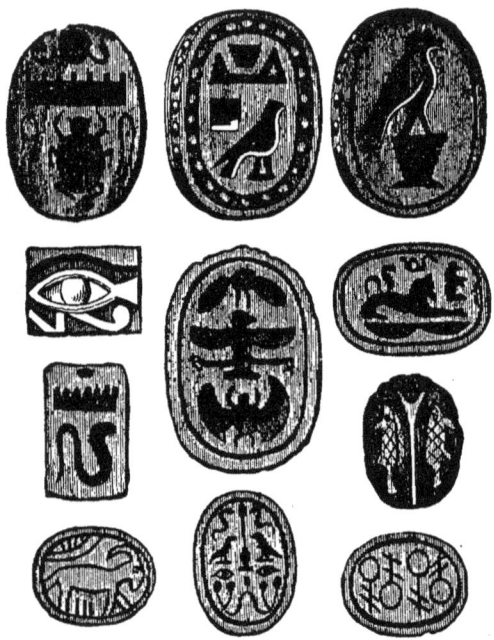

Under-surface of sacred scarabæi, engraven with hieroglyphs.

administered to the unfortunate help who had allowed her to enter. She illustrates the simplicity of these people by the following anecdote:—One day, being more than usually pestered by an Arab trader to buy his genuine antiques, she sharply replied, "I don't like them: I prefer the modern ones." "Bis-allah!" exclaimed the pedlar, "then you will like these; for they were all manufactured by myself."—"As for genuine scarabs of the highest antiquity," says Miss Edwards, "they are turned out by the gross every season. Engraved, glazed, and administered to the turkeys in the form of boluses, they acquire, by the simple process of digestion, a degree of venerableness that is really charming."

Apropos of scarabs, the toleration by Egyptians of all living creatures, from the crocodile to the fly, exhibits, in a high degree, the gentleness and amiability of character of the people. It was not always love—often it was superstition, or fear, that made them so lenient; but, nevertheless, we cannot fail to perceive, in their treatment of animals, a recognition of the rights of all created beings, as well as of themselves. Lady Duff Gordon looked warily around her, lest there should be witnesses, when her prejudices led her to kill a serpent that had intruded itself into her apartment; and she was unable to induce the Arab mothers to kill the gorged flies which hung from the inflamed eyelids of their children afflicted with ophthalmia. The Fellaheen look doubtfully at the sportsman as he fills his bag with the superfluous pigeons, although to themselves they are almost a scourge. Different parts of Egypt preferred different animals, and held them sacred; so that we find a Leontopolis, or city of lions; a Lycopolis, or city of the wolf; a Crocodilopolis, or city of the crocodile; a Bubastis, where the cat was held in veneration; and so forth.

But what shall we say of the venerable scarab, the sacred scarabæus. Those who are sufficiently acquainted with the natural history of certain beetles, are aware that they propel, with their hind-legs, objects of domestic use which they are desirous of storing away in their caves. Now, on the banks of the Nile, the object of greatest importance and anxiety to the scarab is its egg. She lays it near the stream; and, to protect it from injury, she plasters it over with mud, enclosing it like a kernel in its shell; and, instinctively mindful of the rise of the Nile, which would wash it away, she sets herself diligently to work to roll it upward from the river's brink. It has to be propelled often to a considerable distance: she must drive it across the arable belt; for the sepulchre of the scarab, like that of the Egyptian, is the desert; and the male oftentimes helps her in her labour. Arrived at the sandy border of the desert, they dig their well; the precious mummy is deposited therein, to await the return of the spirit of life, and, at the appointed hour, to rise from the tomb into renewed existence. Does not the Egyptian see, in the scarab, the pioneer of his own religious belief?—and hence is led to regard it as the emblem of the divine spirit—the future " to be," or " to transform." Too frequently this labour of love, on the part of the scarab, concludes in sacrifice: the exhausted labourer sinks wearily by the side of the finished tomb, and dies.

Another pleasant sail of 133 miles carries us from Luxor to Syené, or As-souan (Coptic, *souan*, the opening), Egypt's extremest boundary, where Juvenal pined in exile, where the first cataracts burst through the gates of Egypt, and where those grand quarries are stationed which have supplied the whole of the roseate granite obelisks of Egypt. We have already had occasion to mention the existence, in these quarries, of an unfinished obelisk not yet reft from the parent rock, but bearing the traces of the artificers', hands, as though they had unexpectedly been summoned from their work. The dimensions of the Syené obelisk have been variously stated: for example, 100 feet by 11 feet 2 inches; and 95 feet by 11 feet: and a flaw was discovered in the shaft, which has suggested an excuse for its abandonment; while others are of opinion that the flaw is an accident of subsequent occurrence.

The excellence of the quality of the granite of Syené, and its property of splitting under the application of suitable force, permitted the separation from the native rock of a single piece of sixty, seventy, and sometimes more than a hundred feet in length. The unfinished obelisk exhibits the contrivance by which these immense stones were severed from the solid rock. In the course of the line which marks the boundary of the obelisk, is a sharply cut groove; and all along this groove, at short intervals, are holes which are intended for the reception of wedges or plugs of dry wood; when the wedges were driven firmly into the

Mode of Cleaving Obelisks. 123

holes, the groove was filled with water; the dry wedges gradually imbibed the water and swelled, and the force created by their swelling along a line of considerable length, was sufficient to crack the granite throughout the whole extent of the groove. We are but too familiar with this force in the instance of water congealed into ice; a small fissure or opening of any kind becomes filled with water in the winter-time; the water freezes; frozen water expands, and under the force of that expansion the fissure is doubled in extent. It is this process which is so destructive to the face of buildings constructed of laminated stone; it is this which produces the slide of mountains and the fall of cliffs; and the same force the agriculturist utilises by ploughing, for the purpose of breaking up the clods of his land and pulverising the soil. It has been supposed that the Egyptians sometimes had recourse to another method, which is thus described by our old friend, Charles Knight, in the "Pictorial Gallery of Arts."

"One of the modes in which large blocks of granite may be severed from a rock, is exemplified by what takes place in some parts of

India at the present day. The quarryman, having found a portion of the rock sufficiently extensive, and situated near the edge of the part already quarried, lays bare the upper surface, and marks on it a line in the direction of the intended separation, along which a groove is cut with a chisel about a couple of inches in depth. Above this groove a narrow line of fire is kindled, and maintained till the rock below is thoroughly heated; immediately on which a number of men and women, each provided with a vessel of cold water, suddenly sweep off the ashes, and pour the water into the heated groove, which causes the rock to split with a clear fracture. Blocks of granite eighty feet in length are severed by these means." *

From Syené by the cataract or by the road, a short journey of five miles brings us to the lovely island of Philæ reposing in the midst of the placid stream of the Nile, in the golden land of Nubia.† " The approach to the island

* Sir J. F. Herschel's discourse; quoted in Long's "Egyptians," referring to an obelisk erected at Seringapatam.
† The word *noub* signifies gold.

Beautiful Philæ.

by water is very striking. The stream winds in and out among gigantic black rocks of the most fantastic form and shape, and then unexpectedly, after a sharp turn or two, Philæ comes suddenly in sight. 'Beautiful' is the epithet commonly applied to this spot, justly considered to present the finest bit of scenery on the Nile; but the beauty, or rather grandeur, is more in the framework of the picture than in the picture itself. The view from the top of the propylon tower at Philæ, of all beyond the island, is far finer than the view of Philæ itself from any point."* Philæ is outside the natural boundary and proper frontier of Egypt;† and although enriched with a temple dedicated to Isis, its ruins date back no further than the last of the Pharaohs. The Temple of Isis was founded by Ptolemy Philadelphus, and bears the cartouche of Cleopatra; whilst its completion is due to the Roman emperors. Here also may be seen an elegant and picturesque hypæthral, or roofless temple,

* Murray's Hand-book.
† The learned editor of "Murray's Hand-book" observes, that in the Egyptian language the island was called Pilak or Ailak, *the place of the frontier*,—a word perverted by the Greeks into Philæ.

open, as were many of the temples of Egypt, to the blue vault of the firmament. This temple is called "Pharaoh's bed;" but appears to have been the work of the Ptolemies and of the Cæsars.

At the landing-place in front of the chief temple at Philæ, a broad flight of steps, leading upwards from the river's edge, is crowned at the summit by a solitary obelisk, one alone remaining; next follows an avenue of Isis-headed columns, and then the majestic propylon of the temple. The obelisk is of fine sandstone, without sculpture, broken at the summit, and about thirty feet in height. At no great distance is the pedestal, cupped at the top, which formerly supported its companion.

Another obelisk wrought out of red granite is now at Kingston-Lacy, in Dorsetshire, and was brought to England by Mr. William Bankes. It is said to have been carved with the cartouche of Cleopatra, made famous from its furnishing Champollion with two important letters of the hieroglyphic alphabet —namely, K and T—after he had previously gained possession, from the cartouche of

The Philæ Obelisks.

Ptolemy, of the five letters P T L M S. These obelisks are not Pharaonic, but were probably erected by Ptolemy Philadelphus, or by one of his successors. We presume that this latter is the obelisk referred to by Sharpe in the following quotation:—

"We possess a curious inscription upon an obelisk that once stood in the island of Philæ, recording, as one of the grievances that the villagers smarted under, the necessity of finding supplies for the troops on their marches, and also for all the government messengers and public servants, or those who claimed to travel as such. The cost of this grievance was probably greater at Philæ than in other places, because the traveller was there stopped in his voyage by the cataracts on the Nile, and he had to be supplied with labourers to carry his luggage where the navigation was interrupted. Accordingly the priests at Philæ petitioned the king that their temple might be relieved from this heavy and vexatious charge, which they said lessened their power of rightly performing their appointed sacrifices; and they further begged to be allowed to set up a monument to record the grant which they hoped for. Euergetes granted the priest's prayer, and accordingly set up a small obelisk; and the petition and the king's answer were carved on the base."

Mr. Walter Ralph Bankes, of Kingston-Lacy Hall, Wimborne, Dorsetshire, has very kindly furnished us with the following information with regard to the Philæ obelisk, which was brought to England by his relative, Mr. William Bankes:—"The height of the three plinths in one block, on which the pedestal rests, is 2 feet 2 inches; that of the lower member of the pedestal, 3 feet 4 inches; and of the upper member, 2 feet 5 inches; the whole pedestal being one block: the height of the shaft, a monolith, 22 feet $1\frac{1}{2}$ inch; making the entire monument 30 feet $8\frac{1}{2}$ inches. The material of the whole is red Egyptian granite.

"On the foot of the obelisk is inscribed:— 'The granite used in the reparation of this monument was brought from the ruins of Leptis Magna in Africa, and was given for that purpose by His Majesty King George IV.'

"William John Bankes, Esq., M.P., eldest son of Henry Bankes, Esq., M.P., caused this obelisk, and the pedestal from which it had fallen, to be removed, under the direction of G. Belzoni, in 1819, from the Island of Philæ, beyond the first cataract; and brought this platform from the ruins of Hierosyesimnon in Nubia.

" The inscription on this obelisk and pedestal records their dedication to King Ptolemy Euergetes II., and two Cleopatras his queens, who authorised the priests of Isis, in the Isle of Philæ, to erect them about 150 years B.C., as a perpetual memorial of exemption from taxation.

" This spot was chosen, and the first stone of the foundation laid by Arthur, Duke of Wellington, August 17, 1827."

The following is a translation of the three Greek inscriptions on the pedestal of the Egyptian obelisk.

The first two are painted in red letters upon the surface; the lowest is cut into the stone.

Upper Inscription . . . . " of the gods Euergetes . . . . . . gods Epiphanes . . . . . of the gods Eupator, and of the god Philometor, and of the gods Euergetes, greeting.

K

We have submitted to you the copy of the letter written to Lochus, our cousin and general, and we permit to you the setting up of the monument which you apply for . . . . Pacon 22."

Second Inscription.—" King Ptolemy, and Queen Cleopatra the sister, and Queen Cleopatra the wife; to Lochus their brother, greeting . . . to us . . . . . from the . . . . a copy . . . . you shall make . . . not to trouble them " . . .

Third Inscription.—" To King Ptolemy, and Queen Cleopatra the sister, and Queen Cleopatra the wife, beneficent deities; the priests of the great goddess Isis in Abatus and Philæ, greeting. Whereas those frequenting Philæ as generals and prefects and governors of Thebes, and royal scribes, and prefects of the frontier guard, and all other functionaries and constituted authorities, and the rest who are in office, compel us to make contributions to them against our will; and out of this it results that the Temple is deteriorated, and that we are in danger of not having what is appointed for the sacrifices and libations to be made for you and your children.

" We request of you, great deities as you

are, if it shall seem good, to order Noumenius, your cousin and secretary for correspondence, to write to Lochus, your cousin and general of the Thebaid, not to trouble us in these things, nor to suffer any other to do the same, and to give us the necessary decrees to that effect; and in them to permit us to set up a monument, on which we may inscribe your kindness to us upon these points, that your favour may be perpetuated upon it to all time. When this shall be done, we and the Temple of Isis shall hold ourselves obliged. Fare ye well."

It is worthy of remark, that the Egyptian religion, intended to be abolished by Theodosius in his sweeping edict of 381 A.D.,* still existed at Philæ seventy years later— namely, in 453, as is proved by the sculptures on the walls of the temple. And Philæ further claims the honour of being the resting-place of a portion of the body of Osiris, to whom a monolithic shrine, now standing in the sanctuary, is dedicated. Osiris, it will be remembered, was slain by Typhon, or Set, who cut his body into pieces, and dispersed

* Athanasius was patriarch of Alexandria in 327 A.D.

the fragments over the country; so that Philæ is not alone in the possession of so sacred a relic: although Isis, the wife of Osiris, presumedly gathered all the pieces together, when they became united, and Osiris was restored to life. Horus, the son of Osiris, was his father's avenger, and, in his turn, destroyed Typhon. This fable bears several allegorical readings: for example—Osiris, as the setting sun, sinks into the regions of Set, or Saturn, and becomes king of Hades; Isis, or the moon, comes in search of her lost husband; but the sun rises again from the shades of Hades, as Horus, and dispels the darkness of Saturn, and the deadly influences of Typhon.*
This is, perhaps, more obvious if we join with

* Typhon, the genius of evil, is the great ancestor of the too-frequent deadly enemy of our own day, typhus and typhoid fever. In the Egyptian language we meet with many words which are in common use amongst ourselves at the present time:—Chemistry is derived from *Chem*, or *Shem*; *Alabastron*, was a city of Egypt; the Oasis of *Ammon* produces ammonia; the topaz and the sapphire are named after *Topazion* and *Saparine* on the Red Sea; the smaragd, or emerald, is found in Mount *Smaragdus;* and natron and nitre in Mount *Nitria*, &c. So that the world and all its mysteries are but a chain of mutually related links.

the Greeks in calling Horus, Phœbus. Osiris, Isis, Horus, are one form of the Egyptian trinity, in which the humble worshipper of the ancient faith still believes. The trinity was the creed of the earliest family of human beings; and so was the death of one member of that trinity, his descent into Hades, and his subsequent resurrection; with the consequent immortality of the soul. This is all pourtrayed in the Egyptian Triad. Moreover, the name of Osiris among the Egyptians was an unspoken word; it was a holy secret, breathed with extremest caution by the priests themselves. Even Herodotus mentions the word with reluctance; while the most solemn of all adjurations was the name of "him who sleeps in Philæ." Here, then, was a secret, a holy secret, which has descended to Freemasons, and they have since held it, and must ever continue to hold it, sacred.

The decipherment of Egyptian hieroglyphs was a curious accident, and, at the same time, an important step in the science of Egyptology. The French, in the year 1799, while digging the foundation of a fortress at Rosetta, exhumed a slab of black stone—a precious relic, as it proved to be, now carefully preserved in the British Museum.* On this stone was carved an inscription in three languages:—Hieroglyphic, the sacred tongue of Egypt; Demotic, the common language; and Greek. The inscription itself is a decree of the priests in honour of Ptolemy V., Epiphanes. Twenty years elapsed before the value of this writing was realised, although the Greek inscription had not failed to inform its readers that its two companions were translations of itself. The inclusion of royal names and royal titles within an oval had

* In the centre of the southern Egyptian gallery of the British Museum, "is placed the celebrated Rosetta stone; it is a tablet of black basalt, having three inscriptions, two of them in the Egyptian language, but in two different characters (hieroglyphic and enchorial); the third in Greek. The inscriptions are to the same purport in each, being a decree of the priesthood at Memphis in honour of Ptolemy Epiphanes, about the year B.C. 196. This stone has furnished the key to the interpretation of the Egyptian characters." There is likewise, in the same gallery, " a cast of a similar trilingual tablet found at San, being a decree of the priests at Canopus in honour of Ptolemy Euergetes I. and Berenice, B.C. 238." (*Birch.*) San, it will be remembered, is "the field of Zoan of the Bible."

Hieroglyphics Deciphered. 135

been made known by Zoëga some years before; and, comparing the Greek with the hieratic characters, the signs which indicated the name of Ptolemy were next made out. But it did not suffice to identify the emblazonment of Ptolemy alone; it needed the genius of Champollion to discover that the signs represent the letters of the alphabet. The word Ptolemy had supplied him with certain fixed signs, when a happy chance

Cartouche of Ptolemy, or Ptolemais.—The hieroglyphs composing the name are—a square cross-barred, which represents P; a hemisphere, T; a knotted ribbon, O or U; a lion, L; an open quadrangle, M; two leaves of a plant, I or AI; the back of a chair, S; making together, PTOLMAIS; the vowel *e* being lost.

Cartouche of Cleopatra.—The hieroglyphs are — an angle, Q or C; lion, L; leaf, A short, for E; knot, O or U; square cross-barred, P; eagle, A; hand, T; mouth, R; eagle, A; then follow an egg; and a hemisphere t, which indicate sex, and signify daughter. The whole together making CLEOPATRA, a daughter.

presented him with the cartouche of Cleopatra as certified by a Greek inscription on the base of an obelisk from Philæ. Comparing the signs of the two ovals, he was put in possession of three consonants and two vowels, which were identical in both, and corresponded as to position in the construction of the words. The three consonants were P T L, and the vowels E and O. Further research supplied him with the ovals of Berenice, Alexander, Cæsar, Tiberius, Trajan, and Hadrian; which together made up a complete alphabet. He was now in a position to read names in Greek when expressed by hieroglyphic signs. The next step was to convert the signs of the hieroglyphic text into words; and these he found to be Coptic, the national language of Egypt. All this seems to be simple enough when it is known; but Champollion had yet to discover that some of the signs were simply alphabetical, others syllabic, and others again symbolic; moreover, that the three kinds of signs were intermingled, without order, in accordance with the taste of the writer; and that the words were one while abundantly, and another while sparingly, interspersed with symbols. Here the funereal hymns of the Ritual, or Book of the Dead, so often repeated in the papyri, came to his help; for sometimes, in these writings, the words were expressed in symbols, and sometimes in alphabetical signs: the latter disclosed the secret of the former, and so the grammar of hieroglyphography came to be conclusively established. Shall we not, then, in admiration of their fruitful labours, invoke the favour of the Horus, the powerful, the sanctified of truth and wisdom, on these our Egyptographical pioneers, sons of the sun, lords of the diadems, beloved of science, children of genius and industry, establishers of alphabets—the de Sacy, Akerblad, Young, Champollion the resplendent, Lepsius, Hinckes, Brughsch, Saulcy, de Rougé, Birch, the Tum of the western hemisphere, approved of the learned, Bonomi, Tomlinson, and all the rest of the scholarly host, beloved of the birds, which follow in their wake like the stars of the firmament. To all and every, we, lord of the panegyrics, piercer of the sheep, convey our warmest congratulations, veneration, and respect, and wish for them a strong and pure life.

As we float gently away adown the sleepy, stream of the Nile, luxuriating in the dreamy ease of Dahabeeyah life, to our far-away northern and western home, let us try to summarise the results of our exploration into the history of Our Obelisk and its stately family.

I.—USERTESEN I., a Pharaoh of the twelfth dynasty, corresponding with the year 3064 B.C., supplies us with the earliest example of an obelisk, in the venerable monolith still standing at Heliopolis. Its consort is lost, but the pedestal has been recently cleared of rubbish to prove its former existence. The Heliopolis or Matareeah obelisk was originally capped with metal, which has left its mark on the pyramidion; and its shaft is engraven with a solitary column of boldly carved hieroglyphs.

Another quadrangular shaft of syenitic granite, covered with hieroglyphs, and also the work of Usertesen, exists at Biggig in the Fyoom, on the western bank of the Nile, but broken into two pieces. The title, however, of this monument to the rank of an obelisk is a matter of dispute; and for several reasons: first, that it is wanting in the proper proportions of the typical obelisk; secondly, that it is rounded, instead of being pointed, at the apex, and is fashioned in a manner to receive an ornamental finial; and thirdly, and most cogently, that obelisks being consecrated to the rising sun, appertain solely to the eastern bank of the river, whereas this has been set up on the western bank; on which bank it was believed, until quite recently, that no other trace of an obelisk had ever yet been found.

Putting aside the poetical superstition affecting the eastern and western banks of the Nile, and the respective claims of Ra and Tum, the rising and the setting sun, a monolithic shaft, of which the two fragments together measure nearly forty-three feet in length, without accounting for a portion which may have been lost, might, without extreme license, be regarded as an obelisk.* It is true that the apex is rounded; but this may have been the consequence of accident; or

* Sixteen of Bonomi's obelisks have a less altitude than forty-three feet, including two belonging to Rameses II.; two of Psammeticus; the Alnwick obelisk of Amenophis II., so ably described by himself; and the two obelisks of black basalt in the British Museum.

perchance, being the first, or nearly the first, obelisk hewn from the granite rock, it may simply prove evidence of the "'prentice hand," and be merely a ruder example of those more elegant, pointed shafts, which were afterwards to follow. It had a groove on its summit; but this was doubtless to bear a cap, like its big brother at Matereeah; and who knows but that this cap may have completed the point of the rounded head, and, to outward inspection, have made the shaft an obelisk complete. Another allegation against the Biggig monolith is, that it is broader on one side than on the other; but so are the majority of obelisks, as is evinced by our own Cleopatra's Needle; although we are quite willing to confess that the deviation in the candidate before us is more considerable than usual; its mean breadth on two of its sides being 5 feet 2 inches, while that of the other two is 4 feet: its greatest diameter at the base being 6 feet $9\frac{1}{2}$ inches. Under these circumstances it is, that while, by Sir Gardner Wilkinson and M. Mariette, the Biggig monolith is accepted as an obelisk, its privilege to that rank is rejected by Mr. Bonomi.

In a previous page (99) we have alluded to the Temple of Hatasou, at Thebes, on the western bank of the Nile, and consequently its sepulchral side, in the front of which Mariette notes the pedestals of a pair of obelisks. Does not this discovery invalidate, in some degree at least, the theological hypothesis of the rising and the setting sun; the shore of the living, and the shore of the dead? We must confess to considerable hesitation in accepting the sun-theory as an explanation of the site of the obelisks. Nor do we perceive any more reason to assume that a superstitious speculation governed the establishment of the abodes of the living, and of the tombs of the dead, than that the selection was one of simple convenience. The Egyptians are an Asiatic people, and therefore we may presume that they were deeply imbued with theological mysticism from their earliest origin; but, looking upon them in the light of wanderers in search of a home, that word *home*, and its necessities, we should expect to be a stronger and more rational power to govern their choice of residence than the theosophy of their priests. The first monarchical cities of

Egypt, Thinis and Memphis, were founded on the western bank of the Nile; and here likewise sprung up a vast city of tombs. At this early period, the obelisk, the herald of triumph, had not been invented; * it was the manifestation of a more advanced period of social progress, when Thebes had asserted her claim of being the head† place; and, subsequently, at a time when the western shore was deserted by ancient temple-builders, the obelisks followed in the train of the architectural developments of the Theban kings.

* Mr. W. R. Cooper, in his excellent Monograph on "Egyptian Obelisks," just published, makes note of the following curious and interesting quotation from "Letters from Egypt, by Lepsius:"—"A few days ago we found a small obelisk erect, in its original position, in a tomb, near the pyramids, of the commencement of the seventh dynasty (Memphite, 3500—3400 B.C.) It is only a few feet high, but in good preservation, and with the name of the occupant of the tomb inscribed upon it. This form of monument, which is first conspicuous in the new monarchy, is thus removed several dynasties further back, in the old monarchy, even than the obelisk of Heliopolis." This obelisk is remarkable, as having apparently a funereal character.

† Ap, Apé, Tapé, signify, in the Egyptian language, the head or capital of the country; Tapé, in the Memphic dialect, becomes Thaba, which the Greeks have converted into Thebes.

The earliest dynasties were too much occupied with cities, and pyramids, and tombs, to care much for temples and decorative architecture; but Usertesen, whilst he erected temples and obelisks to the sun, likewise excavated tombs on the eastern shore of the Nile; and, as if to exhibit his ignorance of hypothetical sun-worship, planted an obeliskoid monument on the western shore, in the delicious oasis of Fyoom.

Next in the historical series of events followed the five hundred years of stagnation caused by the shepherd invaders; after which, obelisks, delayed for a time, again sprung into existence with the family of their conqueror Amosis, the Amenophs, and the Thothmeses; and once more a contradiction to the sun-theory is presented by not the least distinguished of the last brilliant family, the great Queen Hatasou, or Amun-noohet.

Furthermore, the legend recorded on the fragments of the Biggig obelisk corresponds precisely with that found on the other obelisks. Upon the upper part of this broken monolith, Sir Gardner Wilkinson informs us that there are five compartments, one above the other, in which are represented two figures of the Pharaoh Usertesen making offerings to two deities; below these are hieroglyphs; and on either side of the shaft is a column of hieroglyphs, including a cartouche of the king, on one side describing him as beloved of Ptah, and on the other as beloved of Mandoo.

Mr. Bonomi remarks, that at the time when obelisks first came into use in Egypt, the patriarchs of the Jews were in the habit of setting up large monoliths to perpetuate the memory of great events, and to dedicate the spot to the Almighty. But these stones were taken as they were found, and were unfashioned by the hand of the sculptor; neither were they engraven. The Egyptians likewise set up tables, or tablets, on which legends were engraved; or they carved inscriptions on the rocks. But the Biggig obelisk differs materially from these, as it does likewise from the remarkable, so-called obelisk of Axum. This latter is a very striking and extraordinary monument, and merits exclusion, both on account of its want of proportion, and likewise the absence of written inscriptions. At Axum, the ancient capital of Abyssinia,

Obelisk at Axum.

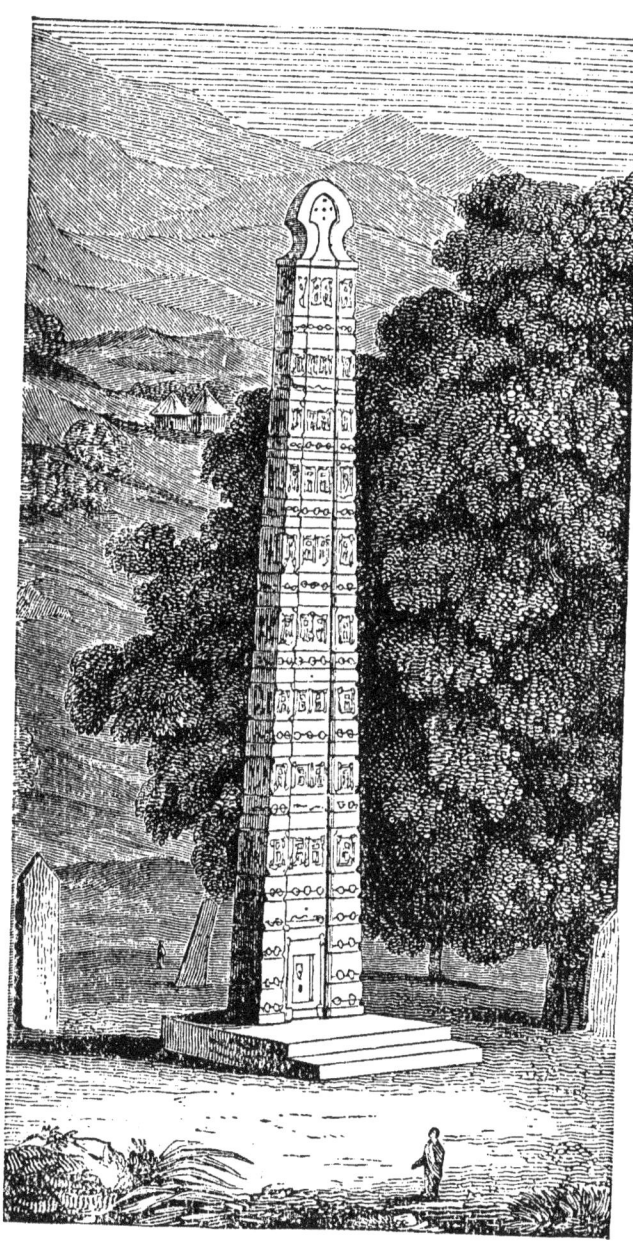

Bruce, the celebrated African traveller, observes:—"In one square are forty obelisks, none of which have any hieroglyphics. There is one, larger than the rest, still standing; but there are two, still larger than this, fallen. They are all of one piece of granite, and, on the top of that which is standing, there is a patera (vase), exceedingly well carved in the Greek taste. Below, there is the door-bolt and lock, which Poncet speaks of, carved on the obelisk, as if to represent an entrance through it to some building behind. The lock and bolt are precisely the same as those used at this day in Egypt and Palestine."

The progress of Egyptological science appears, therefore, to demand that we should adopt the Biggig monolith as a genuine obelisk, however awkward it may be presumed to be in its proportions. It, no doubt, stood once in front of the entrance of a temple dedicated to Ptah, or Vulcan, like the temple of Memphis; and in its broken condition is still highly reverenced by the country-people, who " look on these fragments with the same superstitious feeling as on some stones at the temple of Panopolis, and other places; and the women recite the Fat'ha over them in the hope of a numerous offspring."* That they have some ground for their credence may be gathered from the official legend engraved on the narrow sides, translated by the distinguished Egyptologist, M. Chabas: †—

North.—"The heaven, the kingly Horus, life of *births*, lord of the diadems, life of *births*, king of Upper and Lower Egypt, Ra-kheper-ka, beloved of Ptah of Res-sobt-ef (Ptah of the southern wall), the life of *births*, golden hawk, good god, master of domination."

South.—"The heaven, the kingly Horus, life of *births*, lord of diadems, life of *births*, king of Upper and Lower Egypt, Ra-kheper-ka, beloved of Month, lord of Thebais, life of *births*, hawk of gold, good god, lord of the two lands," . . . .

So long as the Biggig monolith was the only known example of an obelisk on the western shore of the Nile, there were grounds for considering it as an interloper and an im-

---

* Murray's Hand-book.
† "A Short History of the Egyptian Obelisks," by W. R. Cooper, F.R.A.S., M.R.A.S.; 1877.

postor; but at present, since the discovery of the pedestals of obelisks in western Thebes by M. Mariette, it may assert its claim to be admitted into the group of genuine obelisks.

II.—THOTHMES I., of the eighteenth dynasty, which embraces the period between 1703 and 1462 B.C., stands next in age to Usertesen, although about 1,500 years must have elapsed between the dates of their respective works. The obelisk now standing in front of the propylon of the Osiris temple at Karnak, is the work of Thothmes I.; the companion obelisk lies broken by its side. The hieroglyphic exordium of Thothmes I. occupies the pyramidion and two of the faces of the obelisk; while the remaining faces have been appropriated by Rameses II. Two hundred and fifty years therefore must have intervened between the dates of the two writings.

III.—HATASOU, daughter of Thothmes I., erected two obelisks within the temple of Osiris at Karnak, to the honour of her father. Like the preceding, one has fallen to the ground, and one only remains. The standing obelisk is ninety-two feet high,* and is a beautiful work. It is upon the base of this pair of obelisks that we find the legend of their having been hewn from the rock, erected and finished in seven months. The pedestals of two other obelisks are mentioned by Mariette as standing in front of her temple at Deir-el-Bahari, on the western shore of the Nile, at Thebes; but the obelisks themselves are destroyed.

IV.—THOTHMES III. follows next in succession with four obelisks, the four Needles; all erected at Heliopolis; the two beautiful obelisks termed Pharaoh's Needles, and the pair at Alexandria called Cleopatra's Needles. Pharaoh's Needles were removed by the Emperor Constantine; one he conveyed to Constantinople, where it now stands; † and the other was sent to Rome by his son Constantius. The former records the conquest of

* Mr. W. R. Cooper states the height of Hatasou's obelisk as upwards of 97 feet; Lenormant giving it 30 metres (97 feet 6 inches) in altitude, and 368 tons in weight. The height of the obelisk of Thothmes I. is, according to the same authority, 90 feet 6 inches.

† According to Mr. W. R. Cooper, the Constantinople obelisk was brought from Karnak; and sent to Constantinople A.D. 324. It was erected by Theodosius, seventy-three years later—namely, A.D. 397.

Mesopotamia by Thothmes III.; while the latter is the celebrated obelisk of St. John Lateran: besides the cartouche of Thothmes III., it also bears in the lateral columns that

Cartouches of the Pharaoh, Thothmes III.; his prenomen or first or divine name, and his surname or family name; the former being represented by the three syllables; the suns disk, *Ra;* a turreted parallelogram, *men;* and the scarab, *kheper; i.e.,* Ra-men-kheper. And the latter by the sacred Ibis, representing *Thoth,* the god of letters; and the emblem of birth, which stands for *mes;* making together Thothmes.

of his grandson, Thothmes IV.; and of the pair it is said that, unlike the obelisks of Hatasou, they were thirty-six years in the artificers' hands before they were completed. According to Mr. W. R. Cooper, the obelisk at Constantinople " was originally one of the splendours of Karnak." It was broken on its journey to Byzantium; and judging from its present appearance, the upper part alone has been erected. An inscription formerly engraved on its pedestal in Greek and Latin, stated that thirty days were occupied in setting it up, and unpleasantly reminds us of " fire and sword : "—

" I was unwilling to obey imperial masters, but I was ordered to bear the palm after the destruction of tyrants. All things yield to Theodosius and his enduring offspring. Thus, I was conquered and subdued in thirty days, and elevated towards the sky in the prætorship of Proclus."

Of Cleopatra's Needles, one stands at Alexandria; whilst the other, which had fallen several centuries ago, and been buried in the earth, will, we hope, soon fill a site on the banks of the Thames, by virtue of its privilege of being the British obelisk.

Mr. Bonomi admits into his list of obelisks two small granite monoliths dedicated to Thothmes III., which stand before the Usertesen sanctuary at Karnak. " I put them down," he says, in a communication with which he favoured us recently, " as obelisks— because they stand in front of a temple, but doubt their claim to be reckoned such, for they never had the pointed apex. On the north face of the square block are three figures of the Papyrus of Lower Egypt, and, on the south face, three of the Papyrus of Upper Egypt. On the east and west sides are figures of Thothmes embraced by one of the goddesses of Egypt, repeated two or three times. The figures are in the sculpture peculiar to Egypt,* and a little more than three feet high." We entirely agree with Mr. Bonomi, that the monoliths in question, however interesting in other respects, do not come up to the standard of the typical obelisk; and, although occupying so distinguished a place of honour as the front of a sanctuary temple, we must refuse them admission into our present list.

V.—AMENOPHIS II., another Pharaoh of the eighteenth dynasty, is the author of a small, but interesting obelisk, which was brought to England by the Duke of Northumberland (then Lord Prudhoe), in 1838, and now stands in the front hall of Syon House, at Isleworth. It is a monolith of syenite granite, 7 feet $6\frac{3}{4}$ inches in height, supported on a

* The incavo-relievo.

pedestal of 2 feet 8½ inches; making the total altitude of the monument 10 feet 3¼ inches. Its breadth at the base, on two of its faces, is 10⅞ inches, and that of the pyramidion 8½ inches; and, on the adjoining faces, 9⅞ inches, the base of the pyramidion being 8⅞ inches. It therefore happens that the base on two of the sides is only one inch broader than that of the pyramidion; whilst on the other sides the base exceeds that of the pyramidion nearly 2½ inches. The column is broken at the apex, and was found in one of the villages of the Thebaid. This obelisk was made the subject of an interesting paper, published in the "Transactions of the Royal Society of Literature" for 1843, by Mr. Joseph Bonomi, who observes, with regard to it, that it presents the peculiar feature of being inscribed only on one face. Its inscription reads as follows:—

On the *apex*, the god Chnoumis, ram-headed, is seated on a throne; Amenophis II. kneels before him, offering a pyramidal loaf of bread, and says:—"Khnoum, resident in the heart (or centre) of Phi (Elephantine) Ammenhetf (Amenophis II.), giver of life like the sun."

On the *shaft*:—" The Harmachis, the living sun, the powerful bull, the very valiant king of the south and north, Aa-aa-cheferu (prenomen of Amenophis II.), son of the sun, Amenhetf, divine ruler of the Thebaid, has made his offering gift to his father Khnoum (Chnoumis); he has seen given to him two obelisks of the table of the sun (the altar of the sun), that he may make him (the king) a giver of life for ever."

VI.—AMENOPHIS III., also a Pharaoh of the eighteenth dynasty, and the Memnon of the Greeks, erected two obelisks in front of his temple at Karnak. The temple is now a mass of ruins, and the obelisks have utterly disappeared.

VII.—SETI I., or OSIREI, a Pharaoh of the nineteenth dynasty, which ranges in date between 1462 and 1288 B.C., was the author of two, at least, of the obelisks ascribed to his son Rameses the Great. He is said to have been of Semitic origin, and descended from the Hyksos or shepherd kings, and was struck blind at an early period of his career; but having recovered his sight, he devoted himself, for the rest of his life, to the construction of temples and obelisks. Rameses, who delighted in "the bubble reputation," even to his father's loss, inserted his own heraldic bearings on some of Seti's monuments—for example, the Flaminian obelisk, as shown by Tomlinson — and therefore a certain amount of confusion is imported into the differentiation of the works of the two Pharaohs, father and son; although the confusion is at once cleared up when the hieroglyphic writing is investigated. To Seti belong the beautiful Flaminian obelisk at the Porta del Popolo, which is regarded as the first ever removed from Egypt, and that of the Trinita de Monti at Rome.* On these his legend occupies the middle column of the shaft; whilst the titles and praises of Rameses are displayed in the side columns. The Flaminian obelisk was conveyed from Heliopolis to Rome by the Emperor Augustus, as a trophy of war, in the tenth year before the Christian era, and was set up in its present place

* Mr. W. R. Cooper observes, with regard to the Trinita de Monti—"From the style of art in which the characters are cut, it is the general opinion of antiquaries, that the monument is an ancient Roman copy of the larger obelisk in the Piazza del Popolo."

by Pope Sixtus V., in the year 1590. We arrive thus at the number seven for the city of Heliopolis, or more probably *eight;* for, as we now know, obelisks were set up in pairs; and we have reason to regard a city adorned with so many of these emblems of the sun, as very truly the city of the sun. Heliopolis, however, did not possess the greatest number of obelisks, inasmuch as, through the munificence of Rameses II., there were ten or more in the ruined city of San.

VIII.—Rameses II. is the most prolific in the production of obelisks of all the kings of Egypt. The Luxor obelisks owe their origin to him: one is still standing in front of the colossal statues of himself and the magnificent propylon of the great hall of the temple; while

Ovals or Cartouches of Rameses the Great, prenomen and name ; the former signifying Ra-ousor-ma-sotep-en-Ra ; and the latter, Ra-mer-amen, child of the sun.

the other occupies an admirable site in the Place de la Concorde, at Paris.

Two obelisks, bearing his name, ornament the public places at Rome; one in front of the Pantheon, in the middle of a fountain; the other in the garden of the Villa Mattei, on the Cœlian Hill. The former was originally placed in the Circus Maximus, whence it was removed, by Pope Paul V., to the Piazza di S. Martino, and subsequently erected on its present site by Clement XI., in the year 1711; while that of the Villa Mattei, or Cœli Montana, was set up by Pope Sixtus V. in the year 1590. An unlucky incident happened in connection with the latter event; for as the obelisk was being lowered into its place, the architect inadvertently got his hand entangled between its base and the pedestal; and as there was no means of lifting the obelisk, it became necessary to cut off the imprisoned hand at the wrist.

In addition to these four, we must likewise give to Rameses II. the credit of the ten ruined obelisks at Tanis, the field of Zoan; making a total of fourteen. But although, in the gross amount, Rameses II. exceeds all other Pharaohs, he only equals Thothmes III. in the number of the standing ones. Four only of the Rameses obelisks are erect—namely, Luxor, Paris, Pantheon, and Villa Mattei; whilst Thothmes III. equally lays claim to four—Constantinople, St. John Lateran, and the two Cleopatra's Needles.

IX.—MENEPHTAH L, a son and successor of Rameses IL, also of the nineteenth dynasty, is represented as the author of an obelisk which is placed before the front of St. Peter's at Rome. It was brought from Heliopolis to Alexandria by Augustus Cæsar, and afterwards transported to Rome by the Emperor Caligula in the fortieth year of the first century of the Christian era, and marks the period when Peter was released from prison and made his entry into Rome (January 18th, 43 A.D.) The obelisk was erected by Pope Sixtus V., in the garden of the Vatican, in 1586; and is without inscription. It is of this obelisk that the anecdote is told of the almost failure of the operation of erection from the stretching of the ropes. Silence among the workmen had been enjoined under extreme penalties; but a sailor perceiving the difficulty and its cause, suddenly shouted, "Water the ropes." Fontana, the architect, catching the practical force of the suggestion, acted upon it at once, and the danger which had been imminent was averted. Need we say that the sailor was not punished for his infraction of orders, but was handsomely rewarded.

X.—PSAMMETICUS I., a Pharaoh of the twenty-sixth dynasty, corresponding with the year 665 B.C., is the author of an obelisk which was originally erected at Heliopolis, and was brought to Rome by Augustus Cæsar, thirty years before the birth of Christ. It was made to serve the purpose of a gnomon, or pointer, to a great sun-dial in front of the church of St. Lorenzo in Lucina; and was afterwards moved to the Monte Citorio by Pope Pius VI., in 1792. It was found broken into four pieces, and bears marks of extensive repairs.

XI.—PSAMMETICUS II., likewise a Pharaoh of the twenty-sixth dynasty (588—567 B.C.), has his name inscribed on a small obelisk which was set up by Bernini on the back of a marble elephant in the Piazza della Minerva at Rome, by the command of Pope Alexander VII., in the year 1667. It was probably brought from

Sais in the first instance, and was found amongst the ruins of the Temple of Isis and Serapis at Rome. An inscription on this monument reminds the reader, in allusion to the elephant, that a strong mind is needed for the maintenance and exercise of wisdom.

XII.—NECTANEBO I., a Pharaoh of the thirtieth dynasty (378 B.C.), is represented by two small obelisks of black basalt, preserved in the British Museum. Dr. Birch, in a recent communication to us with regard to them, observes, that they were dedicated to the god Thoth, the Mercury of the Greeks, "by a king now recognised as Nekht-her-hebi, the Nectabes or Nekterhebes of the lists; some call him Nectanebo I. They came from Cairo, and formed part of the antiquities surrendered by the French in Egypt after their capitulation, and were presented by George III. about the year 1801." Both have been broken into several pieces, and have lost their summit as well as their pyramidion; their present dimensions being about 8 feet in height, by 1 foot 6 inches on two of the sides, and an inch less on the other two. Bonomi and Cooper, however, attribute them to

Amyrtæus, a king of the twenty-eighth dynasty. Mr. Cooper states that they bear

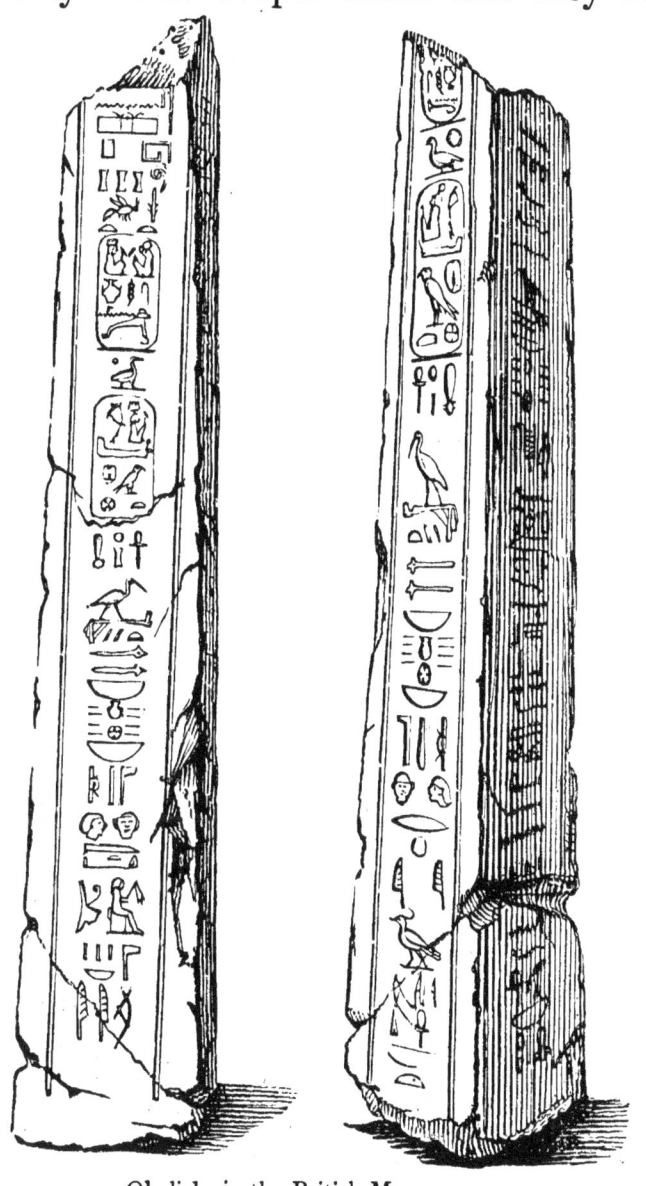

Obelisks in the British Museum.

the cartouche of Amyrtæus, and mentions, as a curious part of their history, that one " was first noticed by Pocock as forming part of a window-sill in the castle of Cairo; and the other, broken in two pieces, was discovered by Niebuhr, one fragment serving as the door-sill of a mosque in the castle of Cairo, while a second was the door-step of a house near Kantara-siedid. . . . The French army of occupation carried off these obelisks from Cairo to Alexandria, and they consequently fell into the hands of the English at the capitulation of that city in 1801. . . . The hieroglyphic inscription has only been partly translated; but the portion so deciphered reads:—' Amyrtæus, the living, like Ra, beloved of Thoth, the great lord of Eshmunayn.' "

XIII.—NECTANEBO II., the last of the Pharaohs, of the thirtieth dynasty, or 378 B.C., is the author of an obelisk without hieroglyphic sculpture, which was set up at Alexandria by Ptolemy Philadelphus, in front of the tomb of his wife Arsinoë. It was subsequently conveyed to Rome, at the command of Augustus, by Maximus, prefect of Egypt, in the tenth year before Christ; and its pyramidion was cut off with the intention of supplying its place with a gilded one: this intention, however, has never been accomplished. It was originally one of the pair, both uninscribed, and both without pyramidion, which were set up before the mausoleum of Augustus in the Campus Martius, and was subsequently placed by Sixtus V. behind the church of St. Maria Maggiore, in 1587. The fellow-obelisk is that now standing in the Piazza Quirinale, on the Monte Cavallo.

Mr. W. R. Cooper remarks, with regard to these two obelisks, that according to tradition, they "were set up at Memphis by King Pepi Merira (Apappus of Eratosthenes), of the sixth dynasty, a monarch who is recorded on the hieroglyphic texts to have reigned for one hundred years, less one hour." They were removed from Egypt to Rome by Claudius Cæsar, A.D. 57, and placed in front of the mausoleum of Augustus. Then sharing the universal fate of all the obelisks at the fall of Rome, they became buried in the earth, and when disinterred had lost the pyramidion, and were otherwise broken. The smaller of the two was dug out by Pius VI. so recently as 1786; "but it occupies, perhaps, a finer position than any of its companions in the city of Rome, except the obelisk of the Vatican, since the architect Antinori erected it on the place of the Monte Cavallo, between the two splendid bronze horses called Castor and Pollux, which once adorned the centre of the Baths of Constantine, and are now the glory of Rome."

In the British Museum, Dr. Birch mentions the existence of a fragment which would appear to be part of an obelisk of Liliputian dimensions. And he further observes that several such small obelisks are known. Mr. Bonomi likewise includes in his list a small obelisk which formerly stood at Constantinople, and quotes from the work of Petrus Gyllus, or Pierre Gilles,* as follows:—

"It is very probable that Constantinople had more obelisks than one. When first I arrived at Constantinople I saw two of them:

---

* Born 1450; died 1555. "Antiquities of Constantinople, written originally in Latin," by Petrus Gyllus, a Byzantine Historian. Translated by John Ball. London, 1729.

one in the Circus Maximus, another in the Imperial Precinct, standing on the north side of the first hill. This last was of a square figure, and was erected near the houses of the Grand Seignor's Glaziers. A little time after I saw it lying prostrate without the Precinct, and found it to be thirty-five feet in length. Each of its sides, if I mistake not, was six feet broad; and the whole was eight yards in compass. It was purchased by Antonius Priolus, a nobleman of Venice, who sent it thither, and placed it in St. Stephen's Market. The other is standing in the Hippodrome to this day." But, according to Long, writes Mr. Cooper, "this obelisk was never removed, but is identical with one of red granite, which still stands in the Sultan's gardens, on the most northern eminence there. From its dimensions, this obelisk is probably of the period of the middle empire; * but as a copy of its inscriptions has not yet reached Europe, or been elsewhere published, all speculation as to its original

* The middle empire is composed of eight dynasties, eleventh to eighteenth inclusive; its date ranges in years between 3064 and 1462 B.C.; and it is made illustrious by the celebrated names of Usertesen, Amenemha, Amenophis, and Thothmes.

place of erection, or the monarch who erected it, would be useless."

Mr. Cooper also includes, in the series of Pharaonic obelisks, a small monolith of sandstone, eight feet in length, which was found by Rüppel lying prostrate on the ground near the wells of Nahasb, in the deserts of Arabia Petræa. The inscriptions on the three sides exposed to the atmosphere are obliterated; but on the under-surface, the hieroglyphs, as far as he could examine them, appeared to be beautifully preserved. The monument was probably of Saitic origin.

Moreover, we must not fail to notice two obelisks, of large size, which were removed from Thebes by the conquering army of Assurbanipal in 664 B.C., and conveyed to Nineveh; where, as they have not since been found, it is to be presumed that they still lie buried in the ruins. "It is not stated from what temple these monuments were taken, and of course it is unknown now, by whom they were erected; but this was the first instance in which an Egyptian obelisk suffered transportation." *

* Cooper.

Obelisks of Philæ. 167

This concludes our survey of the Pharaonic obelisks; and next in order to these follow the obelisks of Philæ, of Ptolemaic origin; the obelisks constructed at the command of Roman emperors, and regarded by *virtuosi* as spurious; and other obelisks of obscure origin. The Philæ obelisks are three in number—the two of sandstone and uninscribed, which stood in front of the Temple of Isis, one of which is still erect, while the other is lost; and a very interesting obelisk of syenitic granite, which was found by Mr. William Bankes and Belzoni among the ruins at Philæ, and was brought to England by Mr. Bankes. This latter is known among Egyptologists as the Corfe Castle Obelisk, and the Soughton Hall Obelisk, although it has never possessed any other site than that on the lawn in front of Kingston-Lacy Hall, at Wimborne in Dorsetshire,* and would more correctly be described as the Bankes obelisk. The Bankes obelisk enjoys the distinction of bearing the cartouches of Ptolemy and Cleopatra, and was one—and a very important one—of the sources

---

* *Vide* Hutchins' edition of Dorset, 1st edition.

whence Champollion drew his interpretation of Egyptian hieroglyphs.

The obelisks constructed by order of the Roman emperors, include those of Domitian, Domitian and Titus, Hadrian, and a small obelisk " executed in Egypt by Santus Rufus .... in honour of one of the Roman emperors .... and afterwards sent to Rome." This is termed the Albani Obelisk, and is now at Munich.*

Domitian's obelisk, also styled the Pamphilian Obelisk, and the Obelisk of the Piazza Navona, in Rome, is erected on a base of rock, forty feet high, in the midst of a fountain, and is ornamented at the four corners with statues of river-gods. It is placed in front of the church of St. Agnes, and is supposed to occupy the spot where that saint suffered her martyrdom. The height of the obelisk is 54 feet 3 inches, and its breadth at the base 4 feet 5 inches. It was set up in its present place by Bernini, in 1651, at the command of Pope Innocent X.

Domitian and Titus are represented in

---

* Cooper; quoted from Westropp's "Hand-book of Archæology." First edition, p. 56.

cartouches on a small obelisk of red granite, a little more than nine feet high, which stands in the Cathedral Square of Benevento. It is carved with several columns of hieroglyphs, but is much mutilated. The inscription records the dedication of a temple to the goddess Isis by the two emperors.* Mr. Cooper, however, takes no notice of a shorter fragment of an obelisk at Benevento, which is set down by Bonomi in his list of erect obelisks.

Hadrian and Sabina are commemorated by an obelisk of red granite, thirty feet in height, which now stands on the Monte Pincio at Rome. It is one of a pair originally planted in front of a temple in the Egyptian city of Antinoopolis, A.D. 131; and records the sacrifice of Antinous, the celebrated favourite of Hadrian. A few years later it was removed to Rome, and erected on the Monte Pincio, where it shared the fate of the rest of the Roman obelisks, thrown down and buried; until, in 1822, it was recovered and set up by Pope Pius VII. " After the erection of this last obelisk," says Mr. Cooper, "no more

* Cooper.

inscribed obelisks were set up, either in Egypt or in Rome. For this there was ample reason: the Egyptian language had been entirely supplanted by the Latin and the Greek; the significance of the characters was unknown; already Pliny had proved his entire ignorance of the script; and Pliny, it must be recollected, was the learned centre of all the science of his time."

Among the obelisks of obscure origin, are a small sandstone monolith, without inscription, in the possession of the Duke of Northumberland, and preserved in the museum at Alnwick Castle; two small obelisks in the museum at Florence; and the obelisk of the city of Arles, on the Rhone.

The two obelisks in the Florentine Museum are only 5 feet 10 inches, and 6 feet high, but differ in breadth, and are the smallest of the obelisk family. They are fashioned of red granite, the pyramidion perfect; but being uninscribed, their authorship and origiu are unknown:

The Arles obelisk, from its position in the city of Arles, on the banks of the Rhone, has suggested the idea that it might have been sent from Egypt to Arles by Constantine, at the time when he was projecting a second Constantinople on that spot; but this illusion is dissipated by the discovery that it is composed of

Obelisk at Arles.

granite of a grey colour, which is found in the neighbouring quarries of Mont Esterel, near Frejus. It is uninscribed, and therefore unable to tell the story of its life; is nearly 57 feet in height, by 7 feet 6 inches in greatest breadth, and "is probably of Roman workmanship." Mr. Cooper remarks, that it must have been left for seventeen centuries on the ground where it was discovered; and, although royal directions were given for its disinterment about the year 1389, it was not until 1676 that it was erected in commemoration of Louis XIV. It is surmounted with a globe representing the earth, and above it a sun: while "beneath the inscription in honour of Louis XIV., is another referring to the late emperor, Napoleon III."*

We have, therefore, brought under our notice a list of thirteen Egyptian Pharaohs (including one Queen), who have left behind them proofs of their taste in the construction of obelisks; namely:—

I. USERTESEN I.; *three*, including the monolith at Biggig; one being lost, one broken, and one remaining entire at Heliopolis.

* Murray's Hand-book for France, 1877.

II. THOTHMES I.; *two*, one broken, the other entire, and known as the small obelisk, at Karnak.

III. HATASOU, Queen; *four*, one broken, two lost, and one, the great obelisk, standing at Karnak.

IV. THOTHMES III.; *four*, all standing, the four Needles; one each in Constantinople, Rome, Alexandria, and London.

V. AMENOPHIS II.; *one*, the Alnwick obelisk, at Syon House, Isleworth.

VI. AMENOPHIS III.; *two*, both broken and lost in the ruins of his temple at Karnak.

VII. SETI I., or OSIREI, the blind king; *two*, both in Rome, the Flaminian and that of Trinita de Monti.

VIII. RAMESES II.; *fourteen*, one each at Luxor and Paris; two in Rome, in front of the Pantheon and in the garden of the Villa Mattei; and ten lost at San, amid the ruins of the "field of Zoan."

IX. MENEPHTAH; *one*, at Rome, the Vatican, before the church of St. Peter; uninscribed.

X. PSAMMETICUS I.; *one*, the "gnomon" obelisk, on the Monte Citorio at Rome.

XI. PSAMMETICUS II.; *one*, the elephant obelisk, in the Piazza della Minerva at Rome, mounted on an elephant.
XII. NECTANEBO I., or AMYRTÆUS; *two*, of black basaltic stone, in the British Museum.
XIII. NECTANEBO II.; *two*, at Rome, both uninscribed; one near the church of St. Maria Maggiore, the other in the Piazza of the Quirinal Palace.

We arrive thus at the number thirty-nine; and if to this number we add the *two* Pharaonic obelisks, Prioli and Nahasb; the *two* Theban obelisks lost at Nineveh; the *three* Ptolemaic obelisks of Philæ; the *four* Roman obelisks of Domitian, Hadrian, and that called Albani; and *five* of obscure origin—namely, the sandstone obelisk at Alnwick, the fragment at Benevento, mentioned by Bonomi, the two Florence obelisks, and the obelisk at Arles—we shall then have a total of fifty-five, of which thirty-three are still standing, and twenty-two have fallen.

We cannot pretend, at this distance of time, to have traced every obelisk issued from the quarries of Syené, to its present resting-place. We know that there were many important cities with their temples in the Delta, now in ruins, their place alone indicated by tumulus-like mounds, where, doubtless, obelisks once stood; nor have we forgotten the fragment which forms part of the pavement of Cairo; nor the hieroglyphed stump on which Pompey's Pillar rests for its chief support at Alexandria. But, strange to say, of the twenty-nine obelisks thus ascertained to be standing, only six remain to Egypt herself— namely, Alexandria, one; Heliopolis, one; Karnak, two; Luxor, one; and Philæ, one.

To the eminent Egyptologist, Mr. Joseph Bonomi,* science is indebted for a list of thirty-two obelisks, arranged in the order of size, and ranging in altitude between 5 feet 10 inches, the smallest of the two obelisks in the museum at Florence; and 105 feet 7 inches, the height of the giant of the obelisk family, that of St. John Lateran at Rome. This latter obelisk has lost nearly a yard from its base in consequence of injury, and would, when perfect, have measured upwards of 108

* "Transactions of the Royal Society of Literature;" second series; vol. i., 1843; page 158.

Altitude of Obelisks.

feet. Mr. Bonomi's list is given in the form of a pictorial diagram, from which we quote the figures as follows:—

	Ft.	In.
1. St. John Lateran, Rome, Thothmes III.	105	7
2. Karnak, Queen Hatasou	93	6*
3. St. Peter's, Rome, plain	88	2
4. Luxor, Rameses II.	—	—
5. Piazza del Popolo, Rome, Seti I.	87	5
6. Paris, Rameses II.	76	0
7. Monte Citorio, Rome, Psammeticus	75	5
8. Karnak, Thothmes I.	—	—
9. Alexandria, Thothmes-Rameses	69	1
10. Heliopolis, Usertesen I.	67	4
11. Arles, France	59	9
12. Navona, Rome, Domitian	54	3
13. Atmeidan, Constantinople, Thothmes III.	50	0
14. St. Maria Maggiore, Rome	48	0
15. Piazza Quirinale, Rome	47	8
16. Trinita de Monti, Rome	43	6
17. Prioli, Constantinople	35	0
18. Philæ	—	—
19. Hadrian, Rome	30	0
20. Corfe Castle, Bankes	22	0
21. Pantheon, Rome	19	9
22. Piazza Minerva, Rome	17	0
23. Alnwick, Syon House	9	0
24. Villa Mattei	8	3
25. British Museum	8	1
26. Florence	5	10

It will be seen that Mr. Bonomi omits to

* *Vide* notes, pages 26 and 149.

mention the height of the Luxor and of the lesser Karnak obelisk: the former appears in his table as fourth in altitude; while its companion, the Paris obelisk, is sixth, with a difference of upwards of ten feet between them. This, if it be so, may possibly result from the removal of some portion of the base of the French monument; although it has been always known that there was some difference of length between them. The smaller Karnak obelisk is about seventy-five feet high. The British obelisk, being prostrate, does not appear in the list; but it has now been ascertained to be taller than its Alexandrian brother, the precise measurements being 68 feet $5\frac{1}{2}$ inches; and 67 feet 2 inches; while the latter is actually shorter, by two inches, than the Heliopolis obelisk. These data serve to place the British obelisk tenth on the list in point of height. Mr. Bonomi's researches likewise direct attention to the following interesting facts in connection with the statistics of obelisks—namely, that out of twenty-one of these Pharaonic monuments, eight possess only one column of hieroglyphs; and in the case of the Alnwick obelisk, only on one side

Distribution of Obelisks.

of the shaft; one, two columns; and seven, three columns; while the remaining five are plain and without any carving at all.

The obelisks at present erect are distributed as follows, age taking precedence in each of the divisions:—

Rome—*Twelve.*

	Ft.	In.
St. John Lateran	105	7
Flaminian, Porta del Popolo	87	5
Trinita de Monti	43	6
Pantheon, Piazza Rotunda	19	9
Villa Mattei, Cœlian Hill	8	3
Vatican, St. Peter's, plain	88	2
Monte Citorio	75	5
Piazza della Minerva	17	0
St. Maria Maggiore, plain	48	5
Piazza Quirinale, plain	47	8
Piazza Navona (Domitian)	54	3
Monte Pincio (Hadrian)	30	0

Italy, in addition to those at Rome—*Four.*

	Ft.	In.
Florence Museum (2)	5	10
Domitian and Titus	9	0
Benevento, fragment	—	—

Egypt—*Six.*

	Ft.	In.
Heliopolis	67	4
Karnak, Thothmes I.	75	0
Karnak, Hatasou	97	6
Alexandria	67	2
Luxor	84	3
Philæ	35	0

Classification of Obelisks.

ENGLAND—*Six*.

	Ft.	In.
Cleopatra's Needle	68	5½
Syon House	8	0
British Museum (2)	8	1
Kingston-Lacy Hall (Bankes)	22	0
Alnwick Castle, sandstone	33	0

FRANCE—*Two*.

Paris, from Luxor	76	6
Arles on the Rhone	56	9

CONSTANTINOPLE—*Two*.

Atmeidan (shortened)	50	0
Prioli	35	0

GERMANY—*One*.

Albani	—	—

Making a total of thirty-three obelisks at present standing.

With one exception, all the known obelisks are Egyptian; hewn by the Egyptians, and from the rocks of Egypt itself, granite, basalt, and sandstone; the exception being that of Arles. Putting, however, the Arles obelisk out of consideration, obelisks admit of being grouped into Pharaonic, Ptolemaic, and Roman; while a sub-group may be formed in each class, consisting of the inscribed and un-inscribed. The inscribed obelisks narrate their own history as if endowed with life; but uninscribed obelisks are mute, and can alone be identified by their surroundings. As it may be convenient to view the obelisks from each of these points of view, we have compiled a few lists, which, we believe, will be found convenient; adopting in every case an order of seniority.

PHARAONIC OBELISKS.

Heliopolis, Usertesen.
Biggig, ditto.
Karnak, Thothmes I.
Karnak, Queen Hatasou.
St. John Lateran, Thothmes III.
Constantinople, ditto.
Alexandria, ditto.
London, ditto.
Syon House (Alnwick), Amenophis II.
Flaminian, Porta del Popolo, Seti I.
Trinita de Monti, ditto.
Luxor, Rameses II.
Paris, ditto.
Pantheon, Piazza Rotunda, ditto.
Villa Mattei, ditto.
St. Peter's, Vatican, Menephtah.
Monte Citorio, Psammeticus I.
Piazza della Minerva, Psammeticus II.
British Museum (two), Nectanebo I.
St. Maria Maggiore, Nectanebo II.
Piazza Quirinale, Monte Cavallo.
Prioli, Constantinople.
Nahasb, Saitic.
Nineveh (two), Theban.

PTOLEMAIC.

Bankes, Kingston-Lacy Hall.
Propylon at Philæ, sandstone.

ROMAN.

Domitian, Rome.
Domitian and Titus, Benevento.
Hadrian, Rome.
Albani, Munich.

UNCERTAIN ORIGIN.

Alnwick Museum, sandstone.
Benevento, fragment.
Florence (two).

FOREIGN.

Arles, France.

UNINSCRIBED OBELISKS.

St. Peter's, Rome, Menephtah.
St. Maria Maggiore, Nectanebo II.
Piazza Quirinale, ditto.
Propylon of Philæ, Ptolemy Philadelphus.
Albani, Munich.
Alnwick Museum, sandstone.
Florence (two).
Arles, France.

The progress of our obelisk to England offers several points of interest which we must leave to another pen than our own to develop.

Before its transport to London became the theme of discussion, there were few probably who cared for it; but since the prospect of its arrival has dawned, many have shown an interest in its disposal. Its earliest friend was the Earl of Harrowby, who considered it worthy of one of the noblest sites in London; and sees in that site a "moral fitness." Indeed, to ourselves, the question is not so much,—Where it will look the best; as, Where it will best be preserved and appreciated:—and we certainly know of no spot in the metropolis so fitting in every respect as St. Stephen's Green, otherwise Parliament Square, with its noble and its venerable monuments and traditions. We could point out many good spots for its erection, but none better; and when the great weight of the monument is taken into consideration, and the obstacles to moving it through a crowded city, we ought to be more than content with the precincts of Westminster Abbey as its ultimate resting-place.

To the son of one who has served his country—to a sailor's son—the Egyptian obelisk illustrates a brilliant bit of British history, of "great events, deeds, and characters" of

British bravery; of VICTORY or WESTMINSTER ABBEY. And of the "moral fitness" of the Westminster site, let us give ear to the gentle teachings of one whose words ought ever to be received with the deepest veneration and respect— Dean Stanley—who, preaching from the pulpit of Westminster itself, on the text—" And who is my neighbour?" illustrating the parable of the Good Samaritan, and the numerous occasions, at home and abroad, on which Christian kindness might be rendered—remarked, the great Egyptian obelisk, now on its way to England, might preach us an useful lesson. " That obelisk," he observes, "if ever it should be planted, will be a lasting memorial of those lessons which are taught by the Good Samaritan. * * * What will it tell us when it comes to stand, a solitary heathen stranger, amidst the monuments of our English Christian greatness—perchance amidst the statues of our statesmen, under the shadow of our legislature, almost within the very precincts of our abbey? It will speak to us of the wisdom and splendour which was the parent of all past civilisation—the wisdom whereby Moses made himself learned in all the learning of the Egyptians for the deliverance and education of Israel—whence the earliest Grecian philosophers and the earliest Christian fathers derived the insight which enabled them to look into the deep things alike of Paganism and Christianity. It will tell us, so often as we look at its strange form and venerable characters, that 'The light which lighteneth every man' shone also on those who raised it as an emblem of the beneficial rays of the sunlight of the world. It will tell us that as true goodness was possible in the outcast Samaritan, so true wisdom was possible even in the hard and superstitious Egyptians, even in that dim twilight of the human race, before the first dawn of the Hebrew law or of the Christian gospel."

So mote it be.

APPENDIX.

OUR narrative of Cleopatra's Needle would be incomplete were we to fail in recording some few memoranda which have fallen in our way, of the personal history of the obelisk: and the first of these to which we shall direct attention is derived from an extract from the *Bombay Courier*, of June 9, 1802, courteously communicated to us by Major-General Bellasis. It runs as follows :—

"The pedestal of the fallen Needle of Cleopatra having been heeled to starboard, and a proper excavation made in the centre of the base stone, this inscription on a slab of marble was inserted, and the pedestal restored to its former situation. The Needle was likewise turned over, and the hieroglyphics on the side it had so long lain on found fresh and entire.

"In the year of the Christian era 1798, the Republic of France landed on the shores of Egypt an army of 40,000 men, commanded by their most able and successful commander, General Bonaparte. The conduct of the general and the valour of the troops effected the subjection of that country. But, under Divine Providence, it was reserved for the British nation to annihilate their ambitious designs. Their fleet was attacked, defeated, and destroyed in Aboukir Bay, by a British fleet of equal force, commanded by Admiral Lord Nelson. Their intended conquest of Syria was counteracted at Acre by a most gallant resistance, under Commodore Sidney Smith; and Egypt was rescued from their dominion by a British army, inferior in numbers, but commanded by General Sir Ralph Abercromby, who landed at Aboukir on the 8th of March, 1801; defeated the French on several occasions, particularly in a most decisive action near Alexandria, on the 21st of that month; when they were driven from the field, and forced to shelter themselves in their garrisons of Cairo and Alexandria, which places subsequently surrendered by capitulation. To record to future ages these events, and to commemorate the loss sustained by the death of Sir Ralph Abercromby, who was mortally wounded at the moment of victory on that memorable day, is the design of this inscription, which was deposited here in the year of Christ, 1802, by the British army, on their evacuation of this country, and restoring it to the Turkish empire."

In the year 1820, we have a more intimate introduction to the obelisk in a very interesting letter from Mr. Briggs, formerly Consul at Alexandria, addressed to the Right Honourable Sir Benjamin Blomfield, one of the ministers of His Majesty George the Fourth.

Letter from Consul Briggs *to the* Right Hon. Sir Benjamin Blomfield.

"Upper Tooting, Surrey.
"11*th April*, 1820.
"Sir,
"Having, on my late visit to Egypt, witnessed the stupendous labours of the celebrated Mr. Belzoni, and received from him the assurance that he could con-

fidently undertake the removal to England of one of the granite obelisks at Alexandria ; and the Viceroy of Egypt, Mahommed Ali Pacha, having frequently expressed to me his desire of making some acknowledgment for the handsome equipment of his corvette, the 'Africa,' and for the presents sent him by His Majesty on the return of that ship to Egypt in the year 1811, I was encouraged to submit to His Highness my opinion that one of the obelisks at Alexandria, known in Europe under the appellation of Cleopatra's Needles, might possibly be acceptable to His Majesty, as unique of its kind in England, and which might, therefore, be considered a valuable addition to the embellishments designed for the British metropolis. His Highness promised to take the subject into consideration ; and, since my return to England, I have received a letter from his Minister, authorising me, if I deemed it acceptable, to make, in his master's name, a tender of one of those obelisks to His Majesty, as a mark of his personal respect and gratitude.

"It is scarcely necessary to say, those obelisks have for ages been admired for their magnitude, workmanship, and antiquity. After the glorious termination of the conjoint expedition to Egypt in 1801, it was proposed by some officers of high rank to convey to England this identical obelisk as an appropriate trophy.

"Representations were actually made, and subscriptions entered into, among the officers of both army and navy; but, being found inadequate, the design was reluctantly relinquished ; and it was generally understood to have been a subject of regret with the administration of that period, that government had been apprised of it too late to afford the necessary means towards its accomplishment.

"Among the officers who had ample opportunities, after the conquest of Egypt, of examining this monument of art, and who may be competent to give a just idea of its merit, may be enumerated, Lord Cavan, Sir Richard Bickerston, Sir David Baird, Sir Hildebrand Oakes, Lord Beresford, Admiral Donelly, and, lately, Sir Miles Nightingale, who visited it on his return from India a few months ago. The two commanders-in-chief of the Egyptian expedition, Lord Keith and Lord Hutchinson, had quitted the country before the plan of removal was in contemplation.

"This obelisk is formed of a single block of red granite (weighing 183 tons, exclusive of the pedestal and steps), originally brought from the quarries in Upper Egypt, near the cataracts. It is now close to the sea-shore at Alexandria, suspended horizontally on its pedestal, in the manner it was placed by our officers in the year 1802, near to the site where the other obelisk is erected. It is about sixty-eight feet in height from the base to the apex, and about seven feet square at the base. On the four sides it is richly sculptured with hieroglyphics in a superior style, more than an inch deep; and though in the lapse of ages it has partially suffered on two sides from the desert winds, the other two are in good preservation.

"The pedestal is a plain block of the same granite, about eight feet and a-half square, and six feet and a-half high. All travellers mention it with encomiums. Clarke, Walsh, and Sir Robert Wilson, lament, in their works, it was not secured to England; and Denon contemplated the feasibility of one day transporting it to France.

"The removal to England of so massive a body would, no doubt, be a work of some difficulty and expense; but similar undertakings have been accomplished by the ancient Romans; and this would have been performed by our countrymen in 1802, had the individual resources of our officers been adequate to the expense.

"In the present state of the arts and sciences in England, it may reasonably be presumed no obstacle can exist but what the munificence of the sovereign can readily surmount. What Belzoni has already done, with only common local means, in conveying to Alexandria, from ancient Thebes, the colossal head which now ornaments the British Museum, together with the success of his other labours, is an earnest of what he is capable of performing; while, at the same time, the unprecedented extent of the excavations attest the liberal character of the present ruler of Egypt, no less than the various improvements he has of late years introduced into the country.

"Eminently brilliant as the government of His Majesty has been, during the Regency, in arms and politics, it will, in future times, be no less distinguished for the liberal encouragement given to the arts and sciences, and for the splendid embellishments conferred on the metropolis. Rome and Constantinople are the only cities in Europe which can boast of Egyptian monuments of this description. They, however, still attest the power and grandeur of the ancient masters of the world; and if the bronze column erected at Paris in modern times serves to ornament that city, and perpetuate the trophies of the French arms, this Egyptian obelisk, in the capital of England, would equally remain a permanent memorial of British achievements, and would be admired by posterity, as well as by the present age, for the boldness of the undertaking as much as for its intrinsic merits.

"I respectfully submit to you, Sir, in the first instance,

this offer of the Viceroy of Egypt, as being in its nature more personal than official, and, therefore, more complimentary to His Majesty. Should you deem it proper to take His Majesty's pleasure thereon, I shall be happy to convey to His Highness the Viceroy the acceptance of his offer, if approved. But should you consider it more correct that I should make this communication to His Majesty's ministers, I shall immediately comply with your suggestion.

"I have the honour to be, with the highest consideration, Sir,

"Your most obedient and humble servant,
"SAMUEL BRIGGS,"
[Formerly Consul at Alexandria.]

We have next to record the unwearied exertions of our kind friend, General Sir James Alexander; to whom we are indebted for our first knowledge that the old Egyptian obelisk was within reach of acquirement by the son of an old naval officer, from whose lips we had often listened eagerly to its praises, and to the narration of the brave deeds of our never-to-be-forgotten heroes, Nelson and Abercromby. Sir James Alexander's communication takes the form of a paper read to the Royal Society of Edinburgh in 1868; entitled, "Observations relative to the Desirableness of Transporting from Alexandria to Britain the Prostrate Obelisk presented to George IV. by Mahommed Ali Pacha." By General Sir J. E. Alexander, K.C.L.S., F.R.S.E., &c.

Transport of the Obelisk.

"In the month of September last (1867), when visiting the Great Exhibition in Paris, I was particularly struck with the fine appearance of the obelisk of Luxor in the Place de la Concorde, and I thought that, as the French had taken the trouble and gone to the expense of moving this highly interesting monolith, it was a reflection on our nation and on the engineering skill of Britain, that the prostrate obelisk at Alexandria (one of Cleopatra's Needles, as it is commonly termed), was not occupying a place of honour in England or Scotland.

"This obelisk was presented to George IV. many years ago by Mahommed Ali Pacha, who also generously offered to move it on rollers to the sea, from which it is 30 yards distant, and, embarking it on rafts and lighters, convey it to a vessel for transport to England.

"The state of public affairs at the time, perhaps, prevented the accomplishment of this enterprise; now the time may be more favourable for it.

"Sir Gardner Wilkinson and other writers on Egypt and its antiquities, are of opinion that Cleopatra's Needles (one of which is upright) were brought by one of the Ptolemies from Heliopolis, near Cairo, to decorate a palace at Alexandria. On the obelisks appear the names of Thothmes III. (B.C. 1463), of Rameses the Great, and of Osirei I. (B.C. 1232), long before Cleopatra's time. Sandys, who travelled in 1610, calls the prostrate obelisk 'Pharaoh's Needle,' and says 'it is half-buried in rubbish.' It is of red granite; and, looking down a hole, its top is seen with crowned hawks sculptured on it. Lord Nugent, writing in 1845, says the hieroglyphics on three sides are well preserved. Colonel Ayton, of H.M. Bombay Engineers, informed me, that whilst in Egypt in 1862, and whilst there was an idea of a memorial for Prince Albert first started, Mr. Clark, of the telegraph department, uncovered the prostrate obelisk, removed the sand and rubbish from it, found the hieroglyphics on three sides in good preservation, and, as the obelisk was not then wanted, he covered it up again.

"This obelisk, with others, is well ascertained to have been quarried at Syené, at the extreme boundary of Upper Egypt. It is not easy to find out how the hieroglyphics were graven on such a hard surface, and what was the process of hardening the bronze tools used for this purpose. The Messrs. Macdonald of Aberdeen, and other workers in granite in this country, might be able to explain this: possibly the assistance of emery-powder was brought in.

"Denon alludes to Cleopatra's Needles, and says they might be moved without difficulty, and form interesting trophies. To remove works of art from countries where they form ornaments, and are conspicuous objects of interest, is quite unworthy of a great people; but the obelisk in question lies in dishonour among low huts in the outskirts of Alexandria, and might well be spared to ornament one of our capital cities. In a conversation with Mr. David Laing, the well-known antiquary, about it, he suggested the open space in front of the British Museum as the most appropriate for it. Still, it might not be sufficiently seen there: further west might be better, or in our Charlotte Square.

"I corresponded with Mr. Newton, the keeper of antiquities, British Museum, about the obelisk; and he writes—'It seems to me that if, by public subscription, a sufficient sum could be raised to transport this obelisk to England, it would be a just matter of national satisfaction; but you will understand that, while this may be a case fully justifying an appeal to the public for a subscription, it may not be one sufficiently strong to justify the trustees and officers of the British Museum in moving in the matter officially, because we have to make so many applications to the Treasury for grants for excavations, &c.'

"I communicated with the Peninsular and Oriental Steam Navigation Company regarding the means of transporting the obelisk; and the secretary for the managing directors states—'We would beg to suggest that the matter should be referred by you to the Foreign Office, whose agents have made all the necessary calculations on the subject, and without whose permission nothing could be done.'

"The Foreign Office was accordingly communicated with, and an answer was returned that the matter is now under the consideration of Lord Stanley.

"The eminent civil engineer, Professor Macquorn Rankine, was asked what he thought of the means of transporting the obelisk, and he said—'I regret I cannot form any opinion whatsoever as to the best way of transporting the obelisk without having detailed information, which, I believe, I could not obtain except by visiting the spot where it lies. The subject is undoubtedly one of very great interest, and I should very much like to be present when it is discussed.'

"In the Royal United Service Institution, London, I found thirteen large plans, carefully drawn, illustrating how, by means of inclined planes, a flat-bottomed vessel, machinery for raising the obelisk on a pedestal, &c., it could be sent to and set up in England. These plans are supposed to have been prepared in 1820, by Captain Boswell, R.N., for the government; but no action was then taken in the matter.

"It appears to me (having studied and been employed formerly as an engineer) that there might be no need for a vessel being built on purpose to carry the obelisk. A large Clyde lighter, raised upon, might transport it across the Bay of Biscay in summer; or, if an old ship, sufficiently seaworthy, is got, and the masts taken out of her, and the beams cut across, the obelisk might be taken alongside, raised, and lowered into her, iron beams being ready, with bolts and screws, to connect and secure the cut beams of the vessel, then towed by a steamer to England. Once there, little difficulty would ensue before it occupied a place of distinction; but not necessarily on a pedestal, which would change its original character through giving it additional height. It is 68 feet long, weighs 184 tons, and is 7 to 8 feet square at the base of the shaft.

"I understand that, in an apartment in the Louvre, part of the machinery is preserved, by means of which the transport of the French obelisk was effected. This could be seen, or even lent to assist our engineers, and save heavy cost; and this need not be heavy, unless with gross mismanagement and a mere job made of it. Honestly gone about, the cost would be moderate.

"Lord Stanley wrote me that he was not aware that the parliament would vote a sum of money to move the obelisk. This might be asked, however.

"I quite concur with Professor Piazzi Smyth in denouncing the barbarism of breaking off pieces of, and carrying away, Egyptian antiques; but I think we might remove the prostrate obelisk hidden and buried in the sand, leaving, of course, the twin obelisk set up in its place, and always most interesting as a 'Cleopatra's Needle.' The prostrate one might be converted into building materials ere long, if not looked after.

"Lately, in Glasgow, I made myself acquainted with the engineer of the Clyde Navigation, Mr. A. Duncan,

I went over the matter with him of the means of transporting the obelisk, and I suggested an iron casing or vessel built round it. He approved of this; and on my asking him to give his ideas on the matter—also to look at the plans from the United Service Institution—he kindly consented to do so; and his clear and excellent method for carrying out what is so much desired—the removal of the obelisk to Britain—is placed before the Royal Society of Edinburgh."

A very important result of Sir James Alexander's agitation of the question, is made evident by the following letter, addressed to Lord Henry Lennox so recently as the spring of 1876 : *—

"Hotel Abbat, Alexandria.
"*April* 1*st*, 1876.

"Dear Lord Henry Lennox,

"A long time has elapsed since our conversation, in July last, with reference to the removal of the obelisk, commonly known as 'Cleopatra's Needle,' as proposed by General Sir James Alexander to the Metropolitan Board of Works. Detained in Persia by an attack of fever, and by unlooked-for difficulties in travelling, I have arrived in Egypt later, by more than three months, than I intended when I left England.

"The taking away of the ancient monuments from a country which they were originally designed to adorn, is a policy against which there is much to be said. It is almost pitiful to contemplate upon the now carefully-protected Acropolis of Athens—a caryatide, rudely carved in wood, doing duty with her four lovely sisters of marble, in

* "Through Persia by Caravan," vol. ii., page 268 : 1877.

bearing the entablature of the Erectheum, while the original is in London instructing the art-world, perhaps no better than would a plaster cast, in the beauty and grace of Greek sculpture. But these considerations do not apply, with any considerable force, to the prostrate obelisk now lying upon the shore of the new port of Alexandria. It forms no part of any structure; it is not protected, nor in any way cared for by the Egyptians; and, within fifty yards of the ground in which the English column is lying, there is another, apparently of the same age and size, carved with hieroglyphics of similar character. It appears to me, therefore, that the English people could, if they please, appropriate this gift free from any fear or feeling that in doing so they would be 'spoiling the Egyptians.'

"The desirability of removing the obelisk resolves itself into two questions—the cost, and the value and interest of the monument as compared with the necessary expenditure. There can be no doubt as to the feasibility of removal. An opinion has certainly prevailed in England that the obelisk is so much defaced and broken as to have lost all interest. But I will venture to say that this opinion has not been formed by any one who has seen the whole of three sides which have been exposed by the excavations recently made by Sir James Alexander. The opinion was formed when but very little more than the upper side of the base was visible—a valueless part which appears never to have been sculptured, and to have been intended for burial in the foundation when the obelisk was in position. The column, as at present exposed, is at once seen to be a monument of great value and interest; one which, not only for its antiquity, but also from its quality as a monolith, would be specially notable in London, which, unlike most of the capital cities of Europe, possesses no adornment of this character. The English people cannot see in their own country a carved stone even approaching the dimensions of this colossal obelisk of red granite. As to the condition of the monument, I have examined three of the four sides, and there is no part of any one of the hieroglyphics the carving of which is not distinctly traceable. The edges of the carving are somewhat worn, and the angles of the obelisk rounded; but the interest of the monument is in no place substantially impaired, nor is there discernable any important fracture of the stone. The dimensions of the obelisk are:—Total length from extremity of base to apex, sixty-six feet; seven feet square at base, and four and a-half feet square at base of apex. The weight is probably about 250 tons.

"In considering the method and cost of removal to England, I have had the great advantage of the assistance, on the ground, of Captain Methven, the senior captain and commodore of the fleet of steam-ships belonging to the Peninsular and Oriental Company. The base of the obelisk is less than twenty yards from the waters of the Mediterranean; and within about 100 yards there is a depth of two and a-half fathoms of water. It has been suggested to float the obelisk by attaching to it a sufficient quantity of timber. But this is a very crude proposal, apart from the fact that no sufficient quantity of timber is obtainable in this almost treeless country. Undoubtedly it would be possible to remove and to ship the obelisk by constructing a railway on piles for such a distance as would admit of the approach of a vessel capable of carrying it securely to England. In this case the obelisk would be suspended in slings from running-gear, and moved out to sea until it hung over its destined position in the vessel. But the shore is not the most suitable for this plan, which, moreover, would involve a very large expenditure.

"The position of the obelisk is favourable for the adoption of a third method, which appears both to Captain Methven and to myself to be the most easy, safe, and practicable; and, at the same time, the least costly of any that have been suggested. The ground in which the obelisk now lies seems sufficiently firm (with proper supports at the sides of the necessary excavation) to sustain girders from which the column could be slung without any change in its position. To ensure a proper distribution of the weight, it would be desirable that these girders should rest on iron plates, and that they should be of greater substance in the centre, where the weight of the obelisk would be borne. Captain Methven is confidently of opinion that the obelisk could be safely conveyed to England in an iron vessel not exceeding 400 tons of builder's measurement, 120 feet in length, and drawing, when loaded, not more than six feet of water. This decked iron vessel, or barge, would be constructed in England, and sent in pieces to Alexandria, where it would be put together in the space to be excavated beneath the suspended obelisk, the channel necessary to get to the deep water being at the same time formed by a steam dredge, or, if the shore is rocky, by blasting—a method which has been very successfully adopted, on a much larger scale than would be requisite here, by the Peninsular and Oriental Company at Bombay. When the vessel was ready to receive the obelisk, the intervening wall of earth between the base of the stone and the sea would be thrown down, and the incoming water would raise the vessel to its burden. The iron barge could then be towed into the harbour, when it would be decked, and have so much freeboard added as appeared desirable. Captain Methven feels quite sure, that by any competent steam-ship of Her Majesty's navy the vessel could be towed to England without danger of damage to the towing-ship, or risk of losing the obelisk, regard being had to the season and to the state of the barometer on quitting this port and that of Gibraltar.

"Finally, I would say that Captain Methven seems to be of opinion that all this could be accomplished at a cost of about £5,000.

"Yours faithfully,

"ARTHUR ARNOLD."

Our memoranda next lead us to the consideration of suggestions which have been made, from time to time, for the transport of the obelisk from Alexandria to England. Thus, in *The Builder* for 1851, vol. v., we find the following communication with respect to two plans proposed by Captain (afterwards Admiral) Smyth.

"One, by building a pier from the immediate vicinity of the obelisk into the little harbour, to the end of which a north-country-built vessel could be brought, with her stern-frame cut out; the obelisk to be conveyed along the pier on rollers in such a manner that half of it should be in the vessel before the weight was felt.

"His other plan was to excavate the ground on which it was lying, so as to form a dry dock beneath; then build under it a lighter, into which the monolith could be lowered, and then letting the water into a canal made to the port to float it away; such vessel subsequently to be towed by a steamer: in either case, the vessel to be properly dunaged with bales of cotton and fascines, so that the Needle, being in midships, would lie easy, and press equally on the vessel's frame. This method is very similar to that mentioned by Pliny."

These several details relating to the British obelisk, naturally awaken our interest to everything bearing upon the subject; and, amongst others, to the method of conveyance of the Luxor obelisk to Paris. Thus, in the "Pictorial Gallery of Arts," we find a description of the transport of the Theban obelisk to Paris, from the pen of our old friend, Charles Knight:—

"The transport of one of these two obelisks to Paris was a very remarkable enterprise. When Napoleon accompanied the French army to Thebes, he was so struck with these magnificent towering masses, that he conceived the idea of sending one of them to France; but his subsequent reverses prevented the idea from being carried out. Thirty years afterwards, Charles X. obtained from Mehemet Ali permission to make the transfer, and he and his successor, Louis Philippe, proceeded with the necessary arrangements. A vessel was built of fir and other light wood, strong enough to bear the sea, but shallow enough to descend the Nile and ascend the Seine. The expedition, comprising about 140 persons, sailed from Toulon in April, 1831, and arrived at Thebes in August of the same year. The difficulties of navigating the vessel up the Nile were very great, and the men suffered much from heat, sand-storms, ophthalmia, cholera, and other visitations of that climate. The officers, on landing at Luxor, superintended the erection of barracks, sheds, and tents; the building of baking-ovens and provision-stores; and the establishment of such arrangements as should ensure the comfort of the men during the operations for the removal of the obelisk.

"The obelisk was upwards of seventy feet high, weighed 240 tons, and was situated 1,200 feet from the Nile, with a difficult intervening space of ground. The first work was the formation of an inclined plane from the base of the obelisk to the edge of the river—a task which occupied about 700 Arabs and Frenchmen for three months. The obelisk was then cased in wood from top to bottom, to prevent the hieroglyphic sculptures from being injured; and it was safely lowered to the ground by a careful arrangement of cables, anchors, beams, and other apparatus. It was lowered on a kind of stage or cradle, and then dragged along the inclined plane by manual labour. The bow end of the ship had been meanwhile cut off in a singular manner, so as to present a wide mouth into which the obelisk gradually glided, while the ship lay high and dry on the sandy shore of the river. The severed bow of the ship was then adjusted in its proper place, and the obelisk was thus housed for the present.

"Although the obelisk was thus placed in the vessel in November, 1831, it was not till August, 1832, that there was sufficient water in the Nile to float it. A period of more than three months elapsed before the adventurers reached the mouth of the Nile, after a voyage of great difficulty and tediousness. The voyage from thence to Toulon occupied them, with various delays, till May. But as the land journey from Toulon to Paris (four hundred and fifty miles) is one which would have been insurmountable with the obelisk, the vessel sailed round to Cherbourg, where it arrived in August, 1834, having been towed by a man-of-war all the way from Egypt. From Cherbourg the vessel was towed to Havre, and from thence by a steam-boat up the Seine to Paris. During the year 1835, preparations were made for the obelisk in the centre of the Place de la Concorde; and in August, 1836, it was placed in the spot destined for it, in presence of the royal family and half the population of Paris."

Another writer, alluding to the same subject in *The Builder* for 1851, vol. ix., also supplies us with interesting details, from personal observation, as to the transport of the Luxor obelisk. He says, that having for some time—

"Considered the matter of bringing the column of Luxor to Paris, and that having reached that city just before the preparations for its erection were finished, and again before the materials had been removed, he can give the following particulars:—

"This monolith stood on the east bank of the Nile, at Luxor, part of the territory or soil of Thebes—famous for its 500 gates; the ancient and celebrated capital of Egypt.

"It was executed about 1,600 years before the Christian era, and about the time of Moses and the exodus of the Israelites, and is consequently about 3,500 years old; though some give it 1,000 or 1,200 years more. It is of reddish Syené granite, beautifully polished, and sculptured with 1,600 figures. The inscription tells us that Pharaoh Rameses II. erected the great northern temple at the palace of Luxor, in honour of his father Ammon.

"It was on a pedestal 3 feet 9 inches high, which was not brought to France.

"England having obtained the fallen pillar, called Cleopatra's Needle, at Alexandria, France demanded, and got the standing one; but those at Luxor being in a perfect state, whilst those at Alexandria had suffered from the climate, France requested, and was allowed to give up, that of Alexandria for that of Luxor.

"Thebes is about 500 miles above Alexandria; and the distance it had to be brought to Paris, including the various detours, is estimated at 3,000 miles.

"The height of the pillar, from the pedestal to the summit, is 75 feet 10 inches. The breadth, on the widest face of its base, 8 feet and a quarter of an inch. The breadth at the top, where the pyramid begins, 5 feet $8\frac{3}{4}$ inches. Its weight, between 250 and 280 tons.

"France had, early in 1830, determined on its removal, and began preparations. A vessel was built of yellow pine strengthened with oak, of 140 feet by 28 feet, like a Dutch galliot, intended to draw only two feet of water. It had a complement of 136 men, including shipwrights, carpenters, masons, and smiths; twelve enormous beams, 75 feet by above 2 feet; deals, blocks, pullies, anchors, and 20,000 yards of the largest and best cordage, &c., &c.

"This vessel, designed by the French government to bring this trophy to France, was built at Toulon, and called the 'Lusquor.' It sailed in March, 1831; arrived at Alexandria in eighteen days, on the 3rd of May, when it entered the old port, and cast anchor under the walls of the palace of Mehemet Ali. It drew nearly nine feet of water, and was a very bad sea-boat, whence arose the necessity of a steamer to tow it home.

"It sailed from Alexandria for Rosetta on the 14th June; it left Cairo, and proceeded up the Nile, on the 19th July, and reached Luxor on the 15th August. At Alexandria the stores and machinery were taken out, and sent forward to Thebes, with carpenters, smiths, masons, and others.

"The obelisk was dismounted from its pedestal on the 31st October, and safely got on board the vessel on the 19th December. Four hundred Arabs were employed with the crew. It required a month to run the obelisk to the ship, being a distance of 450 yards; the greatest difficulty was in keeping it straight on the causeway. It was there detained until the 1st October, 1832; arrived again at Alexandria on the 2nd January, 1833. The fall of the Nile is said to be no more than twenty feet in forty leagues; the rise of the inundation at Luxor, about seven feet. At Rosetta the ship was lightened as much as possible to cross the bay. She was brought down to seven feet, and was in considerable danger; she had camels to assist her. She sailed for France on the 1st of April, and once more reached Toulon on the 1st May, having been towed by the 'Sphynx' steamer, and again sailed for Paris on the 22nd June. During her progress she arrived at Rhodes on the 6th April; reached Corfu the 23rd; 10th May reached Toulon, and was there repaired; 22nd June, sailed; passed Gibraltar the 30th June; and reached Cherbourg on the 12th August.

"At Cherbourg she was visited by King Louis Philippe on the 2nd September.

"She put to sea on the 12th September; was taken in tow by the 'Phœnix,' and reached Rouen on the 14th; and finally arrived at Paris on the 23rd December, 1833. On the 9th August, 1834, the monolith was dragged out of the vessel.

"Thus the 'Lusquor' occupied above four years and a-half, from the commencement of its building to delivering the obelisk at Paris.

"On its arrival at Paris, a wooden erection of similar size, covered with drawings copied from the original, was placed in various parts of the capital, that the best locality for effect might be selected; and the place where it now stands was finally fixed on. Of the propriety of its position there can be no doubt; and when it is considered that the Barriere de l'Etoile cost £400,000, the cost of the obelisk at £85,000 will not appear too extravagant. It was raised on its pedestal on the 25th October, 1834.

"The pedestal on which it now stands was cut from a beautiful black granite rock near Brest, where it is found in the form of large boulders; such boulders being of much finer colour than the black granite formation on which they lie. The property on which the granite was found belongs to M. Bazil.

"It was thus raised:—The column was first carried up an inclined plane to the level of the pedestal, securely placed, the base foremost; and then the pyramid end was raised by an extraordinary multiplication of pullies; and thus was the column lifted into its place.

"And this plan has not improbably been the one adopted in ancient times—perhaps by the Celts and Druids of our own island, who were exceedingly fond of monoliths, of which an astonishing number still remain."

It does not fall within the scope of this book to attempt the panegyric of the brave men who fought like heroes under their country's flag in Egypt; but the following extract from one of the illustrated newspapers, of about the date of April, 1845, and sent to us by the daughter of the subject of the article, may be considered a not unfitting conclusion to our present labours.

"General Robert Browne Clayton, K.C., of Adlington Hall, Lancashire, and of Carrickburn, in the county of

Wexford, entered the army at the early age of fourteen; rose, during sixty years' service, through every gradation of rank; and achieved a well-earned fame by the side of many of the heroes of the late war. He was Lieut.-Colonel of the 12th Light Dragoons, or Royal Lancers. With that regiment he fought in Egypt, under Sir Ralph Abercromby, taking part there in the actions of the 8th, 13th, and 21st of March, 1801."

In his letters home, he speaks with enthusiastic language of Egypt:—"Gizeh," he says, "where the enemy lies, ten miles off; and, across the Nile—Cairo and its lofty minarets, with the dreary Mokattan rising above. In such a situation, one hour of life is worth an age at home; no time or space can efface those recollections. . . . . On our approach to Cairo, which it was expected would be given up to plunder, numerous bodies of Turks and hosts of Bedouin Arabs collected; and I was assured that the Grand Vizier was obliged to issue, daily, 18,000 rations of corn for horses alone."

"The general's patriotic services in the campaign under Sir Ralph Abercromby, have obtained a lasting testimonial in the erection of a lofty column on the rock of Carrick-a-Daggon, county of Wexford. It is a facsimile of Pompey's Pillar, but not monolithic; it consists of Carlow granite, and has a staircase in the shaft: its total height rises to 94 feet 4 inches; the architect is Mr. Cobden. Placed considerably above the sea-level, it stands a conspicuous landmark for mariners. The events of the campaign are further to be commemorated by the appointment of trustees, under the will of General Browne Clayton, who shall annually, at sunrise on the 21st of March (the anniversary of the French attack on the British encampment before Alexandria), hoist the tri-colour French flag on the column, which shall remain until ten o'clock, when the British flag is to be fixed and kept up till sunset. On the 28th of March, annually, the British flag is to be raised half-standard high, as a memorial of the death of Sir Ralph Abercromby. The first commemoration took place in March, 1842, General Browne Clayton himself superintending the ceremony."

The date of General Clayton's death would appear to have been March 16th, 1845; aged 74.

Translation of the Text of the British Obelisk, by DEMETRIUS MOSCONAS: 1877.

Since the final "Revise" of our last sheet, we have received a quarto pamphlet from Alexandria, entitled, "Deux mots sur les Obelisques d'Egypte," with a translation of the inscriptions on Cleopatra's Needle, now on its way to England. The author's name is Demetrius Mosconas; and as the text differs somewhat from that derived from Burton and Chabas, we have thought it well to place it before our readers.

On each side of the pyramidion is a bas-relief of *offerings*, representing the sun-god, protector of the city of On, seated on a throne, adorned with the pschent, or double crown of Upper and Lower Egypt, and receiving gifts from Thothmes, who is represented as a sphynx, symbolising the power of the lion. On the other sides, the sun-god is represented differently: sometimes as a man, crowned with the solar disk; sometimes with the head of a hawk, surmounted with the pschent. And the offerings likewise vary:

they may be wine, or milk, or water, or any other thing that shall in itself be pure and good.

Above the god is inscribed:—

"Ra, the great god, master of the city of On, who giveth eternal life."

Above and below the king, the inscription runs thus:—

"The king, *sun creator of the world* (Ra-men-khéper), lord of Upper and Lower Egypt, the son of the sun, Thothmes, offers libations of wine to him who gives eternal life."

Next follows the standard of the king, and below that, the columns of hieroglyphs; in this instance the middle column representing the address of Thothmes, on the three sides of the obelisk exposed to view:—

1. "He is Horus (Apollo), the powerful bull, friend of truth, the king, *sun creator of the world* (Ra-men-kheper, prenomen), who hath made monuments for his father, the *sun of the two zones*, and who hath erected two great obelisks with pyramidions of gold, which shine with brilliancy at the panegyries . . . . . .

2. "He is Horus, the powerful bull, son of truth, the king, *sun creator of the world*, who hath been established on the throne of Seb by his father, the god Toum, who hath given him the dignity of Thoré, in magnifying his name among the inhabitants of On and of the whole world, the son of the sun, Thothmes, giving life like the sun for ever.

3. "He is Horus, the powerful bull, friend of truth, the king, *sun creator of the world*, the protector of the

Inscriptions on the British Obelisk. 209

temples of the gods, who hath given at every epoch gifts to the divinities of the city of On, and to their servants (the priests); that they may live as saints; moreover, like his grandfather, he hath established numerous festivals; the son of the sun, Thothmes, beloved of the god Toum, *sun of the two zones*, giving life like the sun for ever."

Of the texts of Rameses II., occupying the side columns, the translations of five are given:—

1. "He is Horus, the powerful bull, friend of truth, the king, *sun, guardian of justice, preferred of Ra* (Ra-ouser-ma-sotep-en-Ra, prenomen), the lord of Upper and Lower Egypt; he who governeth Egypt and chastiseth foreign countries, the son of the sun, *Rameses Maïamon*, the ruler and benefactor of the temple of his father, than whom none has done so much as he in this temple, the lord of the two worlds, *sun, guardian of justice, the preferred of Ra*, the son of the sun, *Rameses Maïamon*, who giveth life like the sun for ever.

2. "He is Horus, the powerful bull, son of truth, the king, *sun, guardian of justice, the preferred of Ra*, the lord of the panegyries, like unto his father the god Toum, the son of the sun, *Rameses Maïamon*, the germ of his father whom he loveth, whom the goddess Athor hath nourished, he is the glory and the lord of the two worlds, the *sun, guardian of justice, preferred of Ra*, the son of the sun, *Rameses Maiamon*, who, like the sun, giveth life for ever.

3. "He is Horus, the powerful bull in Egypt, the king, *the sun, guardian of justice, preferred of Ra*, the golden hawk, the guardian of flourishing years, the son of the sun, *Rameses Maïamon*, whose name eternal the puissant of Assyria have graven on their rocks, and in the

temple of his father, the lord of the two worlds, *the sun, guardian of justice, preferred of Ra*, the son of the sun, *Rameses Maïamon*, the truthful, the beloved of the great god Ammon, who giveth life like the sun for ever.

4. "He is Horus, the powerful bull, friend of truth, the king, *sun, guardian of justice, preferred of Ra*, the sublime, the offspring of the gods, the son of the sun, *Rameses Maïamon*, the victorious, the puissant, the watchful, the bull of princes, the king of kings, the lord of the two worlds, the son of the sun, *Rameses Maïamon, the sun, guardian of justice, preferred of Ra*, the beloved of the god Toum, the lord of On, who, like the sun, giveth life for ever.

5. "He is Horus, the powerful bull, son of truth, the king, *sun, guardian of justice, preferred of Ra*, the lord of Upper and Lower Egypt, he who governeth Egypt and scourgeth foreign countries, the son of the sun, *Rameses Maïamon;* numerous victories hath he achieved over foreigners, and he hath carried his conquering arms to the four columns of heaven, the lord of the two worlds, *sun, guardian of justice, preferred of Ra*, the son of the sun, *Rameses Maiamon*, giving life like the sun for ever."

M. Mosconas likewise favours us with part of an heroic poem, translated by Mariette Bey, from a tablet* (stèle) preserved in the Boulaq Museum. This poem is written in honour of the author of the British obelisk, Thothmes III., and is said to be several centuries older than Homer, or even than the Bible. It is regarded by Egyptologists as a precious relic, and as a treasured example of the poetry of that ancient

---

* La Stèle de Phtamosis le Memphite.

Ancient Poem of Phtamosis.   211

period. The Pharaoh presents libations and offerings to the sun-god Amon-Ra, who then recites a long list of the achievements of the king, assuring him of the divine assent, and informing him, that it was to the forethought and participation of the deity that he owed his successes. He speaks thus:—

"Come to me and rejoice in the contemplation of my grace, my son, my avenger. Sun, Creator of the World, living for ever, I am resplendent through thy vows; my heart expands with thy welcome presence in my temple; I embrace thy members in mine arms, that I may infuse into them health and life. Loveable are thy blessings, through the presentment which thou settest up in my sanctuary. It is I who give thee recompense; it is I who give thee power and victory over all nations; it is through me that thy genius and the fear of thy power have taken possession of every land, and its dread hath expanded to the four columns of heaven. I magnify the alarm which thy name inspireth throughout the world. It is with my accord that thy war-cries pierce the very midst of thy barbarian foes, and the kings of every nation fall in under thy hand; I myself stretch forth my arms; I draw together and congregate for thee the Nubians in tens of thousands and thousands, and the northern peoples in millions. It is with my accord that thou hurlest thine enemies beneath thy sandals, that thou smitest the chiefs of the unclean as I have ordered thee; the world, in all its length and breadth, from west to east, is at thy command. Thou spreadest gladness into the heart of all the peoples; none amongst them dare trample on the territory of thy majesty; but I am thy guide to lead thee to them. Thou hast crossed the great river of Mesopotamia, conqueror and mighty, as I had pre-ordered; the cries of war resounded in their caves; I withheld from their nostrils the breath of life. . . .

"I am come, and with my accord thou smitest the princes of Tahi (Syria). I hurl them beneath thy feet when thou marchest through their countries. I have shown them thy majesty as a lord of light; thou beamest upon them like unto mine own image.

"I am come, and I allow thee to smite the dwellers in Asia, to lead into captivity the chiefs of the Rotennu (Assyria). I have revealed to them thy majesty compassed with thy girdle, grasping thy weapon, and wielding it from thy chariot of war.

"I am come, that I might sanction thee to smite the countries of the East, to force thy way to the very cities of the Holy Land. I have revealed to them thy majesty as like unto the star Seschet (Canopus), which darts forth in flame, and gives birth to the morning dew.

"I am come, and I permit thee to smite the countries of the West: Kefa (Cyprus) and Asia tremble with terror in thy presence: I have shown them thy majesty like unto a bull young and courageous; he that, embellished with horns, nothing is able to resist.

"I am come, and I permit thee to smite the peoples of every region; the countries of Maten (Amatuses) shake with the terror of thy name. I have revealed to them thy majesty as like unto the crocodile; he, the formidable master of the waters, whom none dare approach.

"I come, to grant thee permission to smite the inhabitants of islands; the dwellers on the sea-coasts tremble at the sound of thy war-cry; I have shown them thy majesty like unto an avenger who springs upon the shoulders of his victim.

"I come, to permit thee to smite Tahennu (Libyans).

The islands of Tanaou (Danaë) are possessed of thy genius. I have shown them thy majesty as like unto a terrible lion, who maketh his couch of their carcasses, and stretcheth himself across their valleys.

"I come, to permit thee to smite the regions of the floods, that those who abide nigh unto the great sea may be held in subjection. I have made them view thy majesty as of the king of birds, that hovers o'er its prey, and seizes what it lists.

"I come, to permit thee to smite the denizens of the desert, that the Herusha may be brought into captivity. I have made them look upon thy majesty, as like unto the jackal of the day—he that maketh his way in concealment, and travelleth the country through.

"I am come, and I accord to thee the right to smite the Anu of Nubia, that the Remenem (nomad tribes) thou may'st hold in thine hand. I have made them regard thy majesty as like unto those who are thy two brothers, their arms stretched over thee for thy protection." . . .

M. Mosconas' work is illustrated with two pictorial sheets, representing, admirably, every hieroglyph depicted on three of the sides of the British obelisk, with its phonetic equivalent in Egyptian, and its signification in French; the figure and its explanation standing side by side. It is a work which will be found of great value by the Egyptological student, and highly satisfactory to the more learned explorer of hieroglyphography.*

---

* "Deux mots sur les Obelisques d'Egypte et Traduction de l'Obelisque dit de Cleopatre qui doit être transporté en Angleterre et de la Stelè du Phtamosis le Memphite:" par Demetrius Mosconas. Alexandrie, 1877. Quarto, 16 pages, with three Plates.

M. Mosconas alleges that the Alexandrian obelisks were brought from Heliopolis by Cleopatra, and were left neglected for eleven years on the beach of the eastern port of Alexandria; and that they were afterwards erected by Barbarus, Prefect of Egypt, under Augustus Cæsar.

FINIS.

www.ingramcontent.com/pod-product-compliance
Lightning Source LLC
Chambersburg PA
CBHW060836170426
43192CB00019BA/2793